America's Assignment with Destiny

BY

Manly P. Hall

ISBN:978-1-63923-073-0

America's Assignment with Destiny

All Rights reserved. No part of this book maybe reproduced without written permission from the publishers, except by a reviewer who may quote brief passages in a review to be printed in a newspaper or magazine.

Printed August, 2021

Cover Art By: Paul Amid

Published and Distributed By:

Lushena Books
607 Country Club Drive, Unit E
Bensenville, IL 60106
www.lushenabks.com

ISBN: 978-1-63923-073-0

Printed in the United States of America

America's Assignment with Destiny

Foreword

Those desiring substantial evidence of the unfoldment of the Great Plan should follow the suggestion inscribed upon the monument to Christopher Wren in Saint Paul's Cathedral, and gaze about them. The rapid advancement in the social and political states of man, the increasing richness of human living, and the broadening vision toward individual and collective responsibility herald, with auroral colors, the rising sun of truth. There is much yet to be accomplished, but already the achievement is impressive. Even the most devout humanist cannot survey the orderly progress of the race and at the same time deny the existence of a well-integrated program.

The light of the ancient Vedas is slowly but surely illuminating the whole world. The vision of man's noble destiny and the sacred sciences which made possible the realization of that vision have been guarded and served by "the Silent Ones of the earth." The priesthoods of the sacerdotal colleges, the hierophants of the Mystery Schools, and the adept-masters of the Secret Societies have been the guardians of man's noblest

FOREWORD

purpose—the perfection of his own kind. It is the inalienable right of every honorable person to be grateful for the opportunities which progress bestows. With this appreciation comes also an appropriate measure of resolution. The past proves the future, which is but the extension of good works toward their fullness.

The Mystery Schools neither restrained nor limited the unfoldment of human institutions. Man fashioned his civilization according to his natural instincts and convictions. This process must continue, for growth is not hastened by the interference of authority. Man substantiates with his mind and heart that which he fashions with his hands. The esoteric tradition ensouls "the ordinary works," revealing the larger purposes through the smaller ones. No so long ago, ninety percent of the population of the earth was in physical slavery. Having liberated his body, the audacious creature must now free his heart and mind. Thus, pressed on by a sovereign necessity, the world conqueror becomes the self-conqueror.

Under a democratic concept of living, the responsibilities for progress pass to the keeping of the people. The powers vested in the governing body functioning with the consent of the governed include not only provisions for collective security, but also the advancement of such religions, philosophies, arts, and sciences as contribute to the essential growth of human character. An administrative system which ignores ethics, culture, and morality cannot survive as a dominant political organism. Democratic institutions must accept the task for which they were fashioned and become the conscious custodians of the democratic destiny.

Progress demands the most from those with the largest spheres of influence. Vast organizations, industrial, political, social, and educational, have been made possible by the modern life-way. These have become the molders of public opinion, feared or respected according to the measure of integrity revealed in their management. The future of human society is intimately associated with the destinies of these vast enterprises which have inherited, along with physical success, the duty or, more correctly, the privilege of world guardianship. Even the continuance of the economic theory now demands the strengthening of ethical convictions. Prominence of any kind, whether bestowed by wealth or authority, carries with it priestly obligations. The leader, whatever be his field, is looked upon for intelligent guidance. His convictions inspire his followers, his words influence their lives, and his policies dominate their activities.

There is every indication that the esoteric tradition will next function through that complex of vast interrelated organisms of production and distribution which now dominates human imagination. While this structure may appear to the superficial-minded as heartless and soulless, it is also the largest and most powerful potential instrument for the advancement of mankind ever yet devised. Education, science, and economics are today indivisible. They have already formed a partnership for their mutual advancement. Equipped with knowledge, skill, and the necessary physical resources, this huge combine awaits the destiny for which it was intended.

There is no virtue in burdening the future with the conclusions of today. To prophecy is to restrict, not the will of heaven, but the mind of man. Old principles, as they reveal more of themselves, will be given new names; and progress is always an adjustment of concepts, each of which is in a constant state of change. Assuming, however, that the term democracy, with its numerous imponderable overtones, conveys a conviction of natural unfoldment, it is reasonable to infer that the democratic motion will continue until all of its potentials have become potencies.

Progress is not bound inevitably to any nation or people. Social and political structures are instruments for the advancement of the Great Work only to the degree that they keep the faith. If ambition or selfishness breaks the bond, the privilege of guardianship is forfeited. This

FOREWORD

does not mean that the project fails; rather, that which fails the project loses the privilege of leadership. The Plan then passes to the keeping of other groups and other ages. Man cannot destroy or pervert the works of destiny. He can only divide himself from those works, and by so doing cease to share in the essential vitality of progress. Thus it is that unreasonable doubts and fears concerning providence are philosophically unsound. Failure is always regrettable, but principles do not fail, and that which is foreordained perfects itself.

Although empires may collapse, great teachers be martyred, schools and systems perish, the enlightened leaders remain unhonored, the substance of the Great Work remains unchanged and unchangeable. New vehicles appear, even as the older ones are betrayed by human selfishness. The Eternal Commonwealth is an assignment of destiny, and spiritual progress, symbolized by the fabled phoenix, rises victoriously from the ashes of the human ruin. The adept tradition has always available social instruments waiting to be ensouled with the larger vision. All things created by men are mortal and destructible, but the way destined by heaven is immortal and indestructible. Universal enlightenment and universal fraternity are the natural ends which reward the social struggle. The world and all that inhabits it are moving triumphantly toward peace and security. At any given time the vision may be obscured, but in the larger dimensions of time, all things work together for the fulfillment of the greater good.

Manly Palmer Hall
Los Angeles, California
April 1951

Quetzalcoatl

Three great culture heroes were associated with the origin of Mayan civilization: Votan, who founded the Votanic Empire seated at Palanque; Itzama (Zamna), the Yucatecan hero; and Kulkulkan, whose worship extended throughout the Central American area. All three came from a remote region lying eastward, introduced arts and sciences, and founded religious cults or Mysteries. From the legendary histories of these persons, they should be included as adepts or initiates of ancient Secret Schools, possibly Atlantean.

In a book written in the Quichean language and attributed to Votan, the great one declared himself "a snake," a descendent of Imos of the line of Chan. He came to America, by the command of God, from a distant place. He ultimately founded Palanque, and built a temple with many subterranean chambers, which was called the House of Darkness. Here he deposited the records of his nation in the keeping of certain aged men called guardians. There is a legend that this Votan was the grandson of Noah. The original book containing this report was in the possession of Nunex de la Vega, Bishop of Chiapas, but he destroyed it with the other native manuscripts which he was able to accumulate. Fortunately, however, it had been copied by Aguilar.*

—FROM THE *CODEX DRESDEN*

ITZAMNA, THE FATHER OF THE ITZAS
The old god, with elaborate headdress and cape, is seated at right and appears to be addressing a lesser divinity who faces him at left.

Itzamna, according to Cogullodo, was a priest who came with the migrations from the east. He was the son of the supreme deity, Hunab-Ku (the holy one). Itzamna is pictured as an ancient man with a very prominent and strangely shaped nose, either toothless or with one crooked fang. Likenesses of him have been found indicating his birth from a plant growing from the earth. He is also shown rising from the mouth of a serpent or a turtle, to symbolize that he came from the sea. He healed the sick and restored the dead to life. He lived to a great age, and was said to

*See *God of Mexico*, by Lewis Spence.

have been buried at Izamal (Itzamal), where his tombs became places of pilgrimages. Itzamna was sometimes called "the Skillful Hand." After his death, his body was divided. His skillful hand was placed in one temple, his heart in another, and the rest of his remains in a third. One of the best known of his emblems was a Tau or T cross.*

It is now generally admitted that the Quetzalcoatl of the Nahuatlan people, the Gucumatz of the Quiches, and the Kulkulkan of the more southern Mayas were one person. In each language, the word signifies *feathered, plumed,* or *winged serpent.* This title may have resulted from Quetzalcoatl casting his lot among, or gathering his first followers from, the descendants of Votan. This tribal group had the serpent as its heraldic device. At a remote time this semimystical, semidivine priest-initiate Quetzalcoatl came from the fabled land of the "seven colors" and established his rite at Tulla and Cholula.

Quetzalcoatl was the initiate-philosopher and teacher of the Nahuatlan tribes of Central Mexico. Among the appelations of this priest-prophet-king are "he who was born of the virgin," "Lord of the Winds," and "the Divine Incarnation." Quetzalcoatl was the son of the universal creator-god and the virgin Sochiquetzal, and his conception was made known by an ambassador from the god of the Milky Way.

Torquemada, in his *Indian Monarchies,* described a band of people who came from the north dressed in long black robes. Arriving at Tulla, these strangers were well received; but finding the region already thickly populated, they continued to Cholula. These wanderers were great artists, and skilled in working metals. Quetzalcoatl was their leader. Mendieta, in his *Ecclesiastical History,* described Quetzalcoatl as a white man with a strong formation of body, broad forehead, large eyes, and a flowing beard. He wore a miter on his head, and was dressed in a long white robe reaching to his feet, and covered with a design of red

---

*See *Kulkulcan, the Bearded Conqueror,* by T. A. Williard, for further details and pictures.

crosses. In his hand he held a sickle. His habits were ascetic; he never married, and was most chaste and pure in his life, and is said to have endured penance in a neighboring mountain, not for its effect upon himself, but as an example to others. He condemned sacrifices, except of fruit or flowers, and was known as the god of peace; for when addressed on the subject of war, he is reported to have stopped his ears with his fingers.*

Fray Bernardino de Sahagun described Quetzalcoatl as very homely, with a long head and a very long beard. There was a recumbent statue of him in the temple at Tulla which was always covered with blankets. "His vassals," writes the good Fray, "were all workmen in the mechanic arts and skillful in cutting the green stones called Chalchivites, also in the art of smelting silver and making other objects. All these arts had their origin and commencement with Quetzalcoatl, who had houses made with these precious green stones called Chalchivites and others made of silver, still others made of red and white shells, others all made of boards, and again others of turquoises, and some all made of rich plumes. . . .

"Quetzalcoatl also owned all the wealth of the world in gold, silver, and the green stones called Chalchivites, and other precious things; and had a great abundance of cocoa-trees of different colors, which are called xochicacatlao. The said vassals of Quetzalcoatl were also very wealthy, and did not lack anything at all; they never suffered famine or lack of corn; they never ate even the small ears of corn, but rather heated their baths with them, using them instead of firewood. They also say that the said Quetzalcoatl did penance by pricking his limbs and drawing blood, with which he stained the maguey points; that he bathed at midnight in a spring called xicapaya."†

*See *The North Americans of Antiquity,* by John T. Short (New York, 1880).
†See *A History of Ancient Mexico.*

The interpreter of the *Codex Telleriano-Remensis* said that Quetzalcoatl was created by the breath of Tonacatecotli. Quetzalcoatl was born on the day of Seven Canes, and disappeared or died on the day of One Cane. He was identified with the planet Venus. The *Codex Vaticanus A.* says that the hero founded four temples: the first for the princes; the second for the people; the third, the House of Fear or Serpents; and the fourth, the Temple of Shame. The *Codex Chimalpopca* says that Quetzalcoatl was born as a nine-year-old child. When he resolved to leave Mexico, he reached the seashore, and, removing his clothing and his snake mask of turquoise, destroyed himself by fire. His ashes changed into birds, and his heart became the morning star. He remained four days in the underworld and four days as a corpse. After that he ascended to heaven as a god.

It is specifically mentioned by Sahagun that Quetzalcoatl created and built houses under the earth. Traces of subterranean grottoes and rooms have been discovered in the vicinity of most of the architectural monuments of the Nahuas. There is a vast complex of such apartments near the Pyramid of the Sun at San Juan Teotihuacan. The Amerindians believed the serpent to be an earth dweller, and it is quite possible that the accounts implied these subterranean and secret places to be chambers of initiation into the mysteries of the cult. According to de Bourbourg, the Mexican demigod Votan made a journey through a subterranean passage which, running under ground, terminated at the root of heaven. This passage was "a snake's hole," and Votan was admitted because he was himself "a son of the snake."

Quetzalcoatl appeared as the great sorcerer, magician, or necromancer. He performed miracles, and upon his departure his secrets were entrusted to an Order of priests governed by a hierophant or Master. This priesthood practiced the arts and sciences, treated the sick, administered sacraments, and were diviners and prophets. Landa gives some consideration to the activities of these religious Orders.

—FROM SELER'S *CODEX VATICANUS* NR. 3773

Quetzalcoatl as god of the wind and presiding deity over the region of the east.

Lucien Biart summarizes the available data: "The most contradictory ideas have been current in regard to this divinity, who, now considered of celestial origin, and now regarded as a man who had acquired the immortality of the gods, seems in reality to be a union of several personages. . . . He certainly belonged to a race other than the one he civilized; but what was his country? He died, announcing that he would return at the head of white-faced men; and we have seen that the Indians believed his prophecy fulfilled when the Spaniards landed on their shores. According to Sahagun, the most usual ornaments of the images of Quetzalcoatl were a miter spotted like the skin of a tiger, a short embroidered tunic, turquoise earrings, and a golden collar supporting fine shells. The legs of these images were encased in gaiters of tiger-skins, and on their feet were black sandals. A shield hung from the left arm, and in the right hand was a scepter ornamented with precious stones, an emblem which terminated in a crook like a bishop's crosier."*

Quetzalcoatl is credited with the invention of the pictorial or hiero-

---

*See *The Aztecs, Their History, Manners, and Customs* (Chicago, 1929).

glyphical method of writing, and especially is his name associated with the *Tonalamatl,* or *Book of Fate.* This was more than a civil calendar and was reserved for the calculation of human destiny and prophecies concerning the future of the State. It was used by "master magicians," the chief of whom was an astrological adept credited with extraordinary occult powers. While it is likely that Quetzalcoatl brought the *Tonalamatl* back to Mexico after his journey among the Mayas, a people already advanced in such matters, the Aztecan legend has been summarized by Mendieta. The gods had created a man, Oxomoco, and a woman, Cipactonatl, as the progenitors of the human race. They dwelt in a cave at Cuernavaca, and in order to regulate their lives these two resolved to devise a calendar. Cipactonatl felt that her descendant, Quetzalcoatl, should be invited to participate in the project. Because she was the mother of all the living and a great prophetess, Cipactonatl was privileged to select and write the first sign or day-symbol of the calendar. The others followed until the thirteen signs were completed.

Sahagun, in his *General History,* gave a number of details of the struggle between Quetzalcoatl, the civilizer, and Tezcatlipoca, who apparently signified the primitive and sanguine religious cult of Mexico. The old priesthood, which practiced human sacrifice and adhered to a policy of war and destruction, resented the peaceful and gentle faith brought by Quetzalcoatl. In the end, Tezcatlipoca, the personification of the sorcerers, contrived to poison the god-king, which implies that his doctrines were corrupted by false teachings and interpretations.

The poison worked slowly and insidiously, until Quetzalcoatl, realizing that he could not combat successfully the old perverted priesthood, left Tulla, ordering his palaces of gold and silver, turquoise and precious stones to be set afire. Accompanied by a procession of musicians, youths, and maidens bearing flowers, and flocks of singing birds, the old adept journeyed to Cholula, where the great pyramid was built in his honor.

—FROM THE *CODEX RAMIREZ*

Quetzalcoatl as the principal deity of the people of Cholula.

It was written that the Cholulans deeply admired the great priest because of the purity of his life, the kindliness of his manner, and his doctrines of peace and brotherhood. He remained with them for nearly twenty years, slowly sickening from the poison which was destroying his body. At last he realized that his ministry was coming to an end, so he continued his long journey toward the mysterious city of Tlapallan from which he had come. He turned toward the east and proceeded to the sea, which he reached at a point a few miles south of Veracruz. Here he blessed the four young men who had accompanied him and bade them return to their homes, with his promise that one day in the future he would return and restore his kingdom among them.

Then the old and weary man called to the sea, and out of the waters came a raft of serpents. He stepped upon this strange craft and was carried away into the land of the sun's beginning. He left behind him a priesthood that perpetuated with esoteric rites the Mysteries of the Feathered Serpent. There is every indication that the cult of Quetzalcoatl was kept secret, a precaution necessary in the face of the opposition of the primitive indigenous sects.

There are several accounts of the death or departure of Quetzalcoatl. The conflict is due in part to the legends being derived from different tribes, and in part to the Spanish methods of gathering the reports. These invaders took slight interest in the native traditions, until they had destroyed most of the available sources of information. Later, even the converted Indians were uncertain of their tribal history. There is reason to believe, however, that some sacred records were intentionally suppressed and were never available to the missionaries. The people of Mexico claim to have sacred accounts of the mysteries of their religion and the origin of their race. There is mention of the *Divine Book* written by Tezcucan, a wise man or wizard, whose name means Lord of the Great Hand. This was supposed to contain the account of the migration of the Aztecs from Asia. Baron de Waldeck claimed that the book had once been in his possession. De Bourbourg thought it was the *Dresden Codex,* and Bustamante wrote that native historians had a copy in their possession at the time of the fall of Mexico. There is good probability that manuscripts of great value survived the Spanish colonial period and are still available to certain qualified persons.

Augustus LePlongeon, known to the Yucatecans as Great Black Beard, was one of the few Americanists to be accepted into the confidence of the ever-reticent Indians. They told him enough to convince a thoughtful man of the existence of Esoteric Schools in the Mayan area. "That sacred mysteries," writes LePlongeon, "have existed in America from times immemorial, there can be no doubt. Even setting aside the proofs of their existence, that we gather from the monuments of Uxmal, and the descriptions of the trials of initiation related in the sacred book

—FROM AN ORIGINAL PHOTOGRAPH

AUGUSTUS LEPLONGEON

The archaeologist is shown seated among the heads of feathered serpents which he discovered in the ruins at Chichen Itza.

of the Quiches, we find vestiges of them in various other countries of the Western Continent.

"The rites and ceremonies of initiation were imported in Peru by the ancestors of Manco Capac, the founder of the Inca dynasty, who were colonists from Central America, as we learn from an unpublished MS, written by a jesuit father, Red. Anello Oliva, at the beginning of the year 1631, in Lima; and now in the library of the British Museum in London."*

*See *Sacred Mysteries Among the Mayas and the Quiches.*

A number of authors have tried to prove that Quetzalcoatl was a foreigner who, reaching the shores of the New World at an early time, attempted the civilization of the aboriginal tribes. Lord Kingsborough favored the possibility that this wanderer was the Apostle Thomas, and that the ancient Central American Indians came under Christian or Jewish influence.

Always deeply concerned with the possibilities of linking the worship in the Americas with the religions of the Near East, his lordship writes: "The Messiah is shadowed in the Old Testament under many types; such as those of a lion, a lamb, a roe, the morning star (or the planet Venus, otherwise called Lucifer), the sun, light, a rock, a stone, the branch, the vine, wine, bread, water, life, the way, and he is there recognized in the triple character of a king, a priest, and a prophet. It is very extraordinary that Quetzalcoatl, whom the Mexicans believed equally to have been a king, a prophet, and a pontiff, should also have been named by them Ceyacatl, or the morning star; Tlavizcalpantecutli, or light; Mexitli, or the vine (for Torquemada said that the core of the aloe, from which the Mexicans obtained wine, was so called); Votan, or the heart, metaphorically signifying life; and Toyliatlaquatl, *'manjar de nuestra veda,'* bread (for his body made of dough was eaten by the Mexicans)." *

Las Casas, quoting Padre Francisco Hernandez, says that an old Yucatecan described the ancient religion of his people thus: "That [they] recognized and believed in God who dwells in heaven, and that this God was Father and Son and Holy Spirit, and that the Father was called Icona, who had created men and all things, that the Son was called Bacab, and that he was born of a virgin called Chibirias, who is in heaven with God; the Holy Spirit they termed Echuac." The son Bacab was scourged and crowned with thorns, was tied upon a cross with extended arms, where he died; but after three days he arose and ascended into

*See *Antiquities of Mexico.*

heaven to be with his father. Dr. Alexander, who reports this story in his book, is inclined to feel that it is confused and probably distorted by the Spanish recorder. On the other hand, the universal distribution of the basic theme may be explained another way.

Among the Lacandones, Quetzalcoatl is still represented as a snake with many heads. There is an account that this snake was killed and eaten at times of great national peril, especially at eclipses, which were regarded as portents of disaster. It was believed by the Mayas that Kulkulkan descended invisibly from the sky and personally received the offerings during certain great feasts held in his honor. (For details consult *The Mythology of All Ages, Vol. XI, Latin American,* by Hartley Burr Alexander.)

Daniel Brinton, in his *Essays of an Americanist,* devoted some thought to the magical powers attributed to the priests of Central America. He mentioned Father Baeza and an English priest, Thomas Gage, who reported cases of sorcerers transforming themselves into animals, and performing miracles. De Bourbourg was not entirely convinced that ventriloquism, animal magnetism, or the tricks familiarly employed by conjurers explained the mysteries of nagualism, as the black art of these Indians is called. Brinton quotes from the *Popul Vuh:* "Truly this Gucumatz [Quetzalcoatl] became a wonderful king. Every seven days he ascended to the sky, and every seven days he followed the path to the abode of the dead; every seven days he put on the nature of a serpent and he became truly a serpent; every seven days he put on the nature of an eagle and again of a tiger, and he became truly an eagle and a tiger; . . ." It is evident from available authorities that the Mayas and Aztecs had an extensive body of legendry and lore, which originated in the mysteries of their religions and proves the existence of an elaborate system of secret rites and ceremonies.

In the form of a feathered snake, Quetzalcoatl overshadowed a dynasty of rulers and priests, some of whom later assumed his name and even his mask-symbol. These later Quetzalcoatls have been confused, like the several Zoroasters of Persia, into one person, with the resulting conflict in dates. Recent excavations would indicate that the cult of the feathered serpent was established before the beginning of the Christian Era and did not arise in the tenth or eleventh century A.D. as held by some modern archaeologists. It is more likely that the ancient hero was said to have been reborn or to have overshadowed a later leader of the nation.

All the accounts imply that the religious Order which served the Mysteries of Quetzalcoatl was long established. Those who followed in the way which he had prescribed lived most severe lives. Children were consecrated to his temples from their birth and were marked by a special collar. At the end of the second year the child was scarified in the breast. When it was seven years old it entered a seminary where it took vows covering personal conduct and public duties, including prayers for the preservation of its family and its nation. There were many of these priestly Brotherhoods, and the Spanish missionaries, in spite of their theological prejudices and intolerances, were forced to admit that the Aztecan priests were excellent scholars and lived austere and pure lives. It was said of these missionaries that "in Quetzalcoatl, who taught charity, gentleness, and peace, they thought they saw a disciple of Jesus Christ."

The kings of the Mexican nations, like those of ancient Egypt, were also initiates of the State Mysteries. Torquemada described the attainments of Nazahualpilli, the king of Texcuco. This learned man gathered about him masters of the sciences and arts, and gained a wide reputation as an astrologer and seer. When Montezuma was elected to rule over the complex of Nahuatlan nations, King Nazahualpilli stood before the young man and congratulated the entire nation for having selected such a ruler: "Whose deep knowledge of heavenly things insured to his subjects his comprehension of those of an earthly nature."* The interpreter

---

*See Kingsborough's *Antiquities of Mexico.*

of the *Collection of Mendoza* described Montezuma as: "By nature wise, an astrologer and philosopher, and skilled and generally versed in all the arts, both in those of the military, as well as those of a civil nature, and from his extreme gravity and state, the monarchy under his sway began to verge towards empire."

The great serpent clothed in quetzal plumes certainly belonged to another race and came from an unknown country. Lucien Biart says: "It is an incontestable fact that Quetzalcoatl created a new religion, based upon fasting, penitence, and virtue." In skilful trades and in metalworking, this Amerindian savior reminds one of the craftsman of Tyre who cast the ornaments for Solomon's Temple. As a benefactor of his people, as a liberator of men's minds and hearts, this Nahuatlan demigod certainly revealed the attributes of the "Master Builder."

The Mysteries of Xibalba

Scattered through the jungle of Yucatan and extending northward into Chiapas and southward into Honduras and Guatemala are the remains of ancient cities and the ruins of old cultural centers, religious or educational, dedicated to scientific research and the investigation of the spiritual mysteries of human life. These shrines and temples are adorned with numerous religious emblems and figures, and closely resemble the temples and schools of the esoteric tradition which were scattered through the Mediterranean countries, North Africa, and the Near East.

The Aztecs inhabiting the valley of Mexico certainly derived much of their cultural impetus from the more highly civilized Mayas. These Nahuas practiced elaborate rites and ceremonies, and recognized a large pantheon of divinities. It seems unlikely that the Aztecs patterned their religious concepts from some inferior cultural tradition. There are positive indications that the tribes of Central Mexico had received an important intellectual stimulus from the Mayas, and even found it expedient to acknowledge this indebtedness.

The physical remains of the Mayan civilization are sufficiently impressive to indicate a highly advanced people, whose religious institutions and rites had reached a considerable degree of refinement. Most early writers, in an attempt to estimate the cultural attainments of these nations, have been overinfluenced by the early theologians and scientific enthusiasts who invaded the field with a variety of concepts and preconceptions.

—FROM THE *CODEX TROANO*

The black deity holding the spear is believed to represent the hero-god Votan as he appears in the surviving manuscripts of the Mayas.

The empires of the Mayas and Aztecs were resplendent with edifices dedicated to their faiths. There were magnificent shrines, temples, and altars, some to sanguinary deities, and others to benign and kindly gods. The State Mysteries, however, were seldom performed in the sanctuaries of popular worship. Neophytes traveled to remote places, and if they went uninvited, seldom returned. Throughout the jungles are the ruins of extraordinary buildings constructed for unknown purposes.

The Mysteries of Xibalba, as recorded in the *Popul Vuh,* and traditionally associated with the culture-hero Votan, were given in such an architectural complex, which served as an entrance to a mysterious world beyond the dimensions of the material mind.

Such "gateways" existed in all the old countries where the Mystery religion originally flourished. Obviously, archaeologists cannot discover the secret rites merely by grubbing among the overturned and broken stones. As the priesthoods were not considerate enough to label their monuments, there is little left today even to excite curiosity. Fortunately, however, the esoteric tradition survives in the racial subconscious, and its violated schools and colleges need not be physically restored. When such restoration is attempted, the buildings usually reveal that they were designed as symbols of the cosmos.

If the Mystery system existed in the Western Hemisphere, as the landmarks indicate, it must have produced its initiates and adepts. These, in turn, became the leaders and saviors of their peoples. The wonder-working hero, whose deeds enriched all tribal traditions, always and everywhere performed the same miracles, possessed the same powers, and made the same personal sacrifices.

The Mystery School required not only a hierarchy for its maintenance and perpetuation, but also appropriate places of initiation partly underground or adjacent to grottoes and caverns. It required also a body of lore peculiarly significant, participation in which conferred special rights and privileges. A people which had reached the mental platform of the Mayas would not have accepted a philosophy of life that was without profound and significant values. Pagan priesthoods did not initiate those of feeble mind, but selected for spiritual advancement persons of high attainment and mature judgment.

Albert Reville, in the *Hibbard Lectures,* 1894, notes of the religion of the plumed serpent: "There was something mysterious and occult about the priesthood of this deity, as though it were possessed of divine secrets or promises, the importance of which it would be dangerous to undervalue."

It is fortunate, indeed, that at least one manuscript relating to the religious Mysteries formerly practiced in the Mayan area has been recovered. The *Popul Vuh,* or *The Senate Book of the Quiches,* the Record of the Community, has survived the numerous vicissitudes which have conspired to prevent the perpetuation of the literary monuments of Central America. It was tolerated by the early missionaries who, observing certain similarities to their own Scriptures, preserved the work as a means of persuading the Indians to a more speedy baptism. In the seventeenth century, it was rescued from a fate worse than oblivion by the Dominican monk, Don Ramon de Ordonez y Aguiar, dean and chancellor of the archbishopric of Ciudad Real. The work was deposited in the library of the convent at Chichicastenango by its scholiast, Ximenes, where it remained until 1830.

The manuscript of the *Popul Vuh* was rediscovered about 1855 by Dr. Scherzer in the library of the University of San Carlos, Guatemala City. Through the industry and scholarship of that ardent antiquarian, the Abbe Brasseur de Bourbourg, this mysterious book of the Quiches came at last to the French language, where it lingered for years awaiting English translation. Dr. Scherzer was responsible for a Spanish version published in Vienna in 1856. The first English translation has remained practically unknown to students of Central American archaeology, as it appeared serially in *The Word,* a magazine devoted to Theosophical and related subjects. The translation was made by Kenneth S. Guthrie, M.A., Ph.D., M.D., and was based upon the French text.* A new English translation from the Spanish of Adrián Recinos has just been is-

---

*The *Popul Vuh* commenced with the issue of *The Word* for October 1905.

sued by the University of Oklahoma Press. This version is by Delia Goetz and Sylvanus G. Morley, and includes important introductory and commentary material.

Writing under the pseudonym Aretas, James Pryse issued part of the *Popul Vuh* with learned commentaries under the title *The Book of the Azure Veil*. This ran in *Lucifer*, a theosophical magazine, between September 1894 and February 1895. It concluded with a note that circumstances made it impossible for the translator to finish the work.

Pryse suggests that the god Quetzalcoatl was known in Peru under the name of Amaru. He writes: "From the latter name comes our word America. *Amaruca* is, literally translated, 'Land of the Plumed Serpent.' The priests of this God of Peace, from their chief centre in the Cordilleras, once ruled both Americas. All the Red men who have remained true to the ancient religion are still under their sway. One of their strong centres was in Guatemala, and of their Order was the author of the book called *Popul Vuh*."

Although Dr. Scherzer published his copy under the title *Las Historias del origen de los Indios de Guatemala, par el R. P. F. Francisco Ximenes*, this is misleading. Ximenes was not the author, but acted in the capacity of scribe, translator, and commentator. The work is said to have been compiled originally in the seventeenth century by a Guatemalan who had been converted to Christianity. Most American Indians are unsatisfactory converts, for they accept new beliefs without discarding old convictions. This is a most fortunate state of affairs, as there is little indication that the indigenous mythology has been compromised. The source of the material compiled by this convert is completely unknown, but it could well have been derived from a secret book or from oral tradition guarded in the sanctuaries of the Mysteries. To have secured it, the compiler must himself have been a priest or initiate. Certainly, the *Popul Vuh* is by far the outstanding available text on pre-Columbian mythology and cosmogony.

The Quichean scribe, in his introduction to the *Popul Vuh*, writes: "The following is what we shall write, and we place it in writing because, since the 'Word of God' has been promulgated, and hereafter during the cycle of Christianity, the Book of the Azure-green-veil is no longer to be seen, in which it could be clearly perceived that it had come from the further shore of the Sea; which Book has been called 'The Record of our existence in the Overshadowing World, and how we there beheld Light and Life.'" (Note: This translation by Pryse is somewhat fuller than that given by Guthrie, and seems to be more in the spirit of the Quiche tradition.) The implication is that the work originated behind the Azure Veil. This can have two meanings: either the veil which divides the spiritual universe from the material world, or the veil in the temple of initiation, behind which are the Seven Lords of the Great Heart.

The *Popul Vuh* consists of a mythology gradually mingling in its descent with the beginnings of history. The early part deals almost entirely with superhuman beings, and the latter part with the heroic deeds of authentic personages. It opens with a description of the creation. All was calm and silent, and the face of the earth was not yet to be seen. In the eternal darkness and quietude was the Creator—the Lord and Maker—and Gucumatz, the plumed serpent. They were surrounded with green and azure, and they were those who engendered. Then "The Word" came and spake with them, and they joined their counsels. Those who engender then said: "Let it be done. Let the waters retire and cease to obstruct, to the end that it be sown, and that the light of day shine in the heavens and upon the earth; for we shall receive neither glory nor honor from all that we have created and formed until human beings exist, endowed with sentience." Thus the Creator said: "Earth," and immediately it was formed.*

---

*Digested from *The Popul Vuh. The Mythic and Heroic Sagas of the Kiches of Central America*, by Lewis Spence (London, 1908).

The book proceeds much in the spirit of the Scriptures of other nations. It is divided generally into four parts: cosmogony, theogony, anthropology, and regeneration through initiation. It is presented in semihistorical form and includes the initiation of its heroes into the Mysteries of Xibalba.

—FROM SELER'S *CODEX VATICANUS* NR. 3773

REPRESENTATION OF THE BAT GOD FROM THE CODEX FEJERVARY—MAYER 41.

This deity, under the name Camazotz, occurs as Lord of the Bats in the Mysteries of Xibalba.

The heroes of the *Popul Vuh* are subjected to several ordeals or tests of courage, fortitude, and skill. The seventh test took place in the House of the Bat. This was a subterranean labyrinth inhabited by weird monsters and ruled over by Camazotz, a fearful creature with the body of a man and the wings and head of a bat.

Naturally, the account is clothed in the culture symbolism of the Mayas, but it is certainly to be compared with such productions as the Finnish *Kalavala* and the Icelandic *Eddas*. Guthrie presents a number of important parallelisms to the Mysteries of the Egyptians, Chaldeans, and Greeks. According to him, the twelve trials or tests through which the neophytes pass are analogous with the signs of the zodiac. He goes so far as to hazard the speculation that the twelve princes of Xibalba were the rulers of the Atlantean empire, and their final destruction referred to the tragic end of Atlantis.

The *Popul Vuh* follows the traditional form by involving its principle characters in a series of superhuman and supernatural adventures. The work is certainly an account of the "perilous journey," which is the usual means employed to veil thinly the story of initiation. By comparison with the oral traditions of the Northern Amerindian tribes, the legend unfolds what Dr. Paul Radin beautifully calls "the road of light." Medicine priests have freely acknowledged that in dreams and trances they could leave their bodies and travel to the abodes of the gods and the dead. To make this journey while still living is initiation, for it is conscious participation in the fact of immortality.

In some cults the neophyte was given sacred drugs to intensify his psychic faculties, as in the case of the notorious Peyote sect, or was subjected to hypnotic influence, like the followers of the ghost-shirt religion. By some means a condition of death was simulated and the consciousness or superior self passed through certain internal experiences, of which at least a partial memory was preserved.

The entire process of creation took place within the green and azure coils of the plumed serpent. On several continents the serpent was among the important symbols of the initiate-priest. Sometimes the serpent stands erect and is crowned, as in Egypt, or it may be winged as among the Mongolians, or feathered and plumed as throughout the Americas. Obviously, the natives did not intend to imply that they believed in the actual existence of winged snakes, for no such creatures ever existed among them. The serpent was a wisdom symbol, and when plumed it meant that wisdom had been given wings and had become spirit-wisdom, or illumination.

Pryse suggests that Matthew 10:16 explains the symbolism of the snake-bird: "Behold, I send you as sheep [neophytes] into the midst of wolves [the profane]: be ye therefore wise as serpents [magicians], and

—DRAWING BY DR. LEPLONGEON

FEATHERED SERPENT PROTECTING A WARRIOR
An original tracing from the frescoes in the Temple of the Tigers at Chichén-Itzá.

guileless as doves [mystics]." Mr. Pryse was a Greek scholar and his translation differed slightly from the King James Version. He felt that the quetzal had the same meaning as dove, and that the creature combining the serpent-wisdom and the bird-intuition or -inspiration represented the adept, in whom the mind and heart doctrine were completely reconciled.

The conflict between the initiate and the adversary, or the paths of white and black magic, is always present. In the story of Deganawida, the power of evil was personified by Atotarho, an old war chieftain, who had a cluster of venomous serpents on his head in place of hair. The Mexican Quetzalcoatl was attacked by the red god of war. The adversary personified either older cults which opposed the establishment of the benevolent Mysteries or later cults responsible for the destruction of these institutions. In either case an inferior state of spiritual enlightenment was implied. The Mysteries were institutions of liberation and were naturally opposed by groups seeking to keep their people in bondage through ignorance. The struggle was, therefore, between religion as temporal authority and the Mystery faith—the internal "road of light." The ruins of the past explain why it was the common belief that the men of good spirit, the initiates, were sacrificed to the material ambitions of temporal rulers.

American Indian Mysticism

All the aboriginal tribes of North America practiced mystical and magical rites, and vestiges of an esoteric tradition, served by a priestly class distinguished for sagacity and personal integrity, are still to be found among surviving groups. Scattered over a vast area and divided further by lack of a common language, these nomadic bands were approaching the horizon of national existence when the European colonists conquered their lands, decimated their tribes, and destroyed their cultural patterns. So diversified were the traditions of these peoples that it is difficult to summarize their beliefs and doctrines, especially after their legends, histories, and religious institutions were corrupted by outside influences.

The European colonists were of no mind to search for the mystical secrets of the Indian "life-way." These settlers brought their own religious beliefs, which they were resolved to force upon the natives. There were no ethnologists or anthropologists among the Puritans, and many important landmarks of Indian philosophy were destroyed before they had been honestly investigated or appraised. Most of the tribal lore was in the keeping of priests and elders, and if these were killed or died without finding suitable successors the traditions ended. Even today older Indians find it difficult to select younger men to perpetuate the sacred institutions. Thus it is unwise to assume that from available fragments a complete picture of Indian mysticism can be reconstructed.

The Indian has always been an individualist, and neither circumstance nor inclination induced him to form extensive intertribal organizations. His way of life and the vast silences of his homeland caused him to turn within himself for courage, wisdom, and faith. He could not visit distant shrines of learning or sit at the feet of famous teachers. There were no books to ponder and no ancient sages to guide his religious convictions. Few strangers visited his camp with news or opinions from far places. He was part of a small family, and the tribal life, with its simple lore, was his only source of cultural tradition.

A thoughtful observer of Nature about him, the Indian lived constantly in the presence of mysteries, with no reference frame other than his own imagination. Though stoical in appearance, he was highly emotional, as indicated by his songs, dances, and festivals. His sensory perceptions were acute, and his legends indicate strong dramatic instincts.

Among advanced tribes, according to Dr. Franz Boas: ". . . an elaborate series of esoteric doctrines and practices exists, which are known to only a small portion of the tribe, while the mass of the people are familiar only with part of the ritual and with its exoteric features. For this reason we often find the religious beliefs and practices of the mass of a tribe rather heterogeneous as compared with the beliefs held by the priests. Among many of the tribes in which priests are found, we find distinct esoteric societies, and it is not by any means rare that the doctrines of one society are not in accord with those of another. . . . Esoteric forms of religion in charge of priests are found among the tribes of the arid region of the Southwest, the tribes of the southern Mississippi basin, and to a less extent among the more northerly tribes on the Plains. It would seem that, on the whole, the import of the esoteric teachings decreases among the more northerly and northeasterly tribes of the continent."*

The medicine priests were trained by their predecessors or were called to their life work by some miraculous incident. The little Indian boy who early in life showed a tendency to dreams and visions was encouraged to select this career. In a highly organized tribal system, he was initiated into the religious institutions of his nation, receiving the lore of the old priests and fragments of tribal history. If he belonged to some small, wandering band, his entire spiritual education had come from within and was induced by fasting and vigil. The vigil was the most widely practiced religious discipline of the Amerinds. In all matters of emergency or great decision the Indian sought solitude. He went alone to some high place, built a small campfire, planted about him a circle of prayer plumes, smoked the ceremonial pipe, and waited through the long hours of the night for the "voices."

—FROM EMERSON'S *INDIAN MYTHS*

AMERINDIAN PICTOGRAPH OF MANABOZHO, THE
GOD OF LIGHT AND THE HERO-FRIEND OF MANKIND

*See *Handbook of American Indians*, Smithsonian Institution, Bulletin 30, article "Religion."

The "voices" instructed him in the herbs of healing, taught him the songs and dances, and brought him news of what was transpiring in distant places. There are many stories about medicine priests learning to leave their bodies at will and journeying into the shadowland to guide the dying to the home of ghosts. Many of these grand old mystics were wise in the ways of the spirit, and should be regarded as duly initiated members of Esoteric Orders.

The miraculous powers of the medicine priests extended over a wide variety of phenomena. They healed the sick, protected their tribes, directed the migrations of their peoples, and sought by extrasensory means the location of food, water, and other necessities. They predicted the future, induced rain and storms, projected themselves to distant places, and read the hearts and minds of their fellow men. It was in their power to induce visions and trances, and to receive the impressions of the star-spirits. They also gained considerable proficiency in the mesmeric and hypnotic arts.

Charles F. Lummis, who spent many years among the Southwest Indians of the United States, described the miracles performed by the medicine priests. Although naturally skeptical, his experiences among the Navajo and Pueblo Indians impressed him deeply. Mr. Lummis mentioned how Indians seated in their medicine lodge created miniature thunderstorms within the room, accompanied by flashes of forked lightning, while the outside sky was entirely clear. He says: "How the effects are produced I am utterly unable to explain, but they are startlingly real." He was also impressed by the ability of the priests to change themselves into animals in the presence of spectators. Some priests could create an artificial sun inside the lodge. This miniature luminary rose in the eastern side of the room, crossed overhead, and set in the west during the performance of the sacred chants.

Amerindian priests grow the sacred corn in exactly the same way that the East Indian mendicant grows his mango tree. The magician plants the seed which grows immediately, and about three hours later the stalk is laden with fully developed ears of corn.

Other writers have reported that in some of the medicine lodges the Indians are able to levitate large stones and to cause their own bodies to float in the air. Unprejudiced observers have been forced to conclude that among most tribes of Amerinds magical rituals are performed involving the use of natural forces beyond the normal experience of human beings.*

The Amerindic concept of cosmogony paralleled, in a general way, that of the Chaldeans and other peoples who dwelt in the valley of the Euphrates. The world consisted of three regions, with human beings inhabiting the surface of the central zone. Above this middle land was an airy expanse extending to the abode of the Sky-Father. Below the surface were subterranean levels extending downward to the place of the earth-mother. This cavernous region was like the dark and shadowy underworld of the pre-Homeric Greeks.

In the Southwest legends, human beings originated beneath the earth in a kind of paradisiacal land. There, also, were mountains, valleys, and beautiful plains, and a sun and moon that lighted the region. In the beginning everyone was happy, but later an evil deed brought upon them the wrath of the gods. In most accounts this lovely shadowland was destroyed by a flood. In some miraculous manner a few righteous persons were preserved and took refuge on a tall plant, which, growing rapidly, finally broke through the surface of the middle land, bringing the survivors to safety.

The secrets of healing, prophecy, and magic came to the Indian from an order of beings called *manitos*. This Algonquian word is now applied to the concept of powerful governing spirits. The *manitos* were not actually gods, but superhuman manlike creatures, possessing ex-

---

*See *Some Strange Corners of Our Country*, by Charles F. Lummis.

—FROM LUMMIS'S *STRANGE CORNERS OF OUR COUNTRY*

Navajo Indian magicians growing the sacred corn.

traordinary attributes and frequently considered as giants. The size factor, however, is figurative rather than literal. The *manitos* were a divine invisible tribe—masters of magic—to whom human beings could turn for help and guidance whenever necessity arose.

The effort to explain the term *manito* as only signifying a "wonderful power" and synonymous with the Iroquois *orenda* is not sufficient to meet the requirements of the Indian religious philosophy. Orenda conveys more precisely a power or energy universally present in animate and inanimate creatures, and manifesting through the vital processes which cause things to exist, to function, and to affect other existing and functioning things. It might be safer to assume that the *manitos* represented the intelligence controlling and directing the "wonderful power." The Indian, therefore, was confronted with the same basic question which disturbs even the most advanced physicist, namely: Is there a supreme intelligence governing universal procedure?

"The religious concepts of the Indians," writes Dr. Boas, "may be described in two groups—those that concern the individual, and those that concern the social group, such as tribe and clan. The fundamental concept bearing on the religious life of the individual is the belief in the existence of magic power, which may influence the life of man, and which in turn may be influenced by human activity. In this sense magic power must be understood as the wonderful qualities which are believed to exist in objects, animals, men, spirits, or deities, and which are superior to the natural qualities of man."*

Most religions and metaphysical philosophies include hierarchies of divine creatures, or tutelary spirits, as mediators between the Supreme Being and mortals. The *manitos* acted as wise distributors of the *orenda*. The Indian fashioned these demigods in his own likeness, but bestowed upon them superior powers. The *manitos* were aware of the most secret human thoughts and the most pressing human needs, and were capable of responding immediately to the rituals of the priests and elders. When the medicine man journeyed to the spirit land, he might be invited to attend a council of *manitos*. When he came to the Great Lodge in the sky, it resembled an earthly council place, except that it was larger, more elegant, and usually filled with a strange light. The *manitos* were venerable sachems, usually handsome old men, their faces full of kindness. There was a council fire, the smoking of the calumet, and the usual speeches and discussions. The Lodge was a kind of superphysical senate where all matters of grave import were decided. When the session was concluded, the priest returned to his people along the "sky road" and reported the decisions of the Great Lodge.

Between the *manitos* and mankind were the souls of the illustrious dead. These were the Olds and the Trues, the sages of long ago, the great chieftains, warriors, and statesmen. They had led their people in life, so they continued to guard them from the other land, speaking through the

---

*See *Handbook of American Indians*, Smithsonian Institution, Bulletin 30, article "Religion."

medicine men. It seemed natural to the Amerinds that the heroes who had gone before should continue to serve the tribes they had guided in the long ago.

Totemism was a kind of heraldry among the Indians. The totem was the clan symbol; but more than that, it was a channel for the distribution of *orenda* through the social and political structure of the clan. The totemic animal or bird was a spirit guardian, helpful because the creature possessed attributes superior in some particular to those of man. The attribute might be swiftness, strength, cunningness, or resourcefulness, and these qualities the totem creature shared with those under its guardianship. Each Indian also had his own totem, and while it took a familiar form it was identical in principle with the guardian daemon described in works on the Egyptian and Chaldean Mysteries. It was considered a good omen to see one's totem while practicing vigil, or in dreams or trances. It proved the proximity of a protecting power.

The Abbé Phavenet, a missionary to the Algonquians, identifies the totem (from *ote,* the *ototeman* of the Chippewas) with the *manito* concept in these words: "It is to be presumed that in uniting into a tribe, each clan preserves its *manitou,* the animal which in the country whence the clan came was the most beautiful or the most friendly to man, or the most feared, or the most common; the animal which was ordinarily hunted there and which was the ordinary subsistence of the clan, etc.; and this animal became the symbol of each family and that each family transmitted it to its posterity to be the perpetual symbol of each tribe [clan]." Modern ethnologists have emphasized that the popular usage of the term *totem* is incorrect. The symbol is not strictly religious, but involves a social and family concept with emphasis upon the importance of kinship.

Many tribes, especially the Plains Indians, believed that thunder and lightning were caused by enormous birds—the rumbling sounds in the sky accompanying storms were due to the flapping of their wings, and the flashes of light were caused by the opening and closing of their eyes. In some groups, only one thunderbird was recognized; in other tribes, there were several of various colors or a family of them. The appearance of the bird, or birds, is not definitely given; it might be similar to a large hawk, an eagle, or even a grouse. The thunderbird could use its wings as a bow to shoot arrows, and small meteors were believed to be the heads of these arrows. On the Plains, thunderstorms were said to result from a contest between a thunderbird and a huge rattlesnake, or dragonlike monster. Persons struck by lightning, if they recovered, were accepted as sages or holy men, having received a very strong medicine from the experience.

In some areas the thunderbird was closely associated with the religious Mysteries or Societies. Those who saw this creature in their vigils usually considered themselves as intended for a religious life. The myths and legends of the thunderbird are similar to the European and Asiatic accounts of the fabled phoenix, which nested in flames and symbolized initiation and adeptship. Early drawings of the Great Seal of the United States indicate that the bird represented thereon was a phoenix rather than an eagle. Like the Mexican coat of arms, which shows an eagle with a serpent in its claws, the American device is strongly reminiscent of a thunderbird. These creatures were also said to inhabit a sky-world above the clouds, and served as messengers between mortals and the heavenly beings.

Farther south the thunderbird symbol merged with the quetzal and the serpent feathered with quetzal plumes. The quetzal was identical in meaning with the phoenix of Asia, North Africa, and the Near East. The feathered-serpent symbolism can be traced back to the hooded Nagas, or serpent gods of India, and to the winged serpents which occur in the writings and sculpturings of the Egyptians.

The serpent was the messenger and servant of the earth-mother because it dwelt below ground. For this reason rattlesnakes were released during the snake dances, in order that they might carry the petitions of the tribe to the mother who dwelt below. Birds were also carriers of tidings, and as they flew upward they bore with them prayers to the Great Father who lived in the Sky-Lodge. The thunderbird was the most powerful and was the lord of flying things. The thunderbird and the feathered snake were symbolic of the mysteries of the upper and lower regions. Priestly Orders served this twofold cult, the secrets of which were revealed only by an internal mystical experience.

Brinton, describing various devices used by the Amerindian tribes to conserve their religious secrets, says: "All these stratagems were intended to shroud with impenetrable secrecy the mysteries of the brotherhood. With the same motive, the priests formed societies of different grades of illumination, only to be entered by those willing to undergo trying ordeals whose secrets were not to be revealed under the severest penalties. The Algonkins had three such grades, the *waubeno,* the *meda,* and the *jossakeed,* the last being the highest. To this no white man was ever admitted. All tribes appear to have been controlled by these secret societies."*

Among the Amerindians, Secret Societies existed for the perpetuation and enlargement of the choicest knowledge of the tribe. There were war associations, healing cults, and Fraternities concerned with the religious Mysteries, the keeping of records, and the dramatization of myths. There were ethical societies, orders of mirth-makers, fire-walkers, and hunters, presided over by elders who had distinguishing regalia. Women frequently became leaders of these groups. Among the Pueblo Indians there were often a dozen or more Societies in one village. While their objectives were not always parallel, there was no friction between the memberships and they united in all common responsibilities.† The Indian was always a tolerant man on the subject of spiritual convictions. He

---

*See *Myths of the New World* (New York, 1876).
†See Dr. John Swanton, in *Handbook of North American Indians,* article "Secret Societies."

never inquired as to the faith of his guest, but expected that every true believer would conduct himself in an honorable way. He respected the rites of strangers, and if he did not share in them or did not understand their meanings, he kept a respectful silence.

The reference to the dramatization of myths suggests that a number of Indian tribes were practicing the same methods of presenting religious Mysteries that were employed by the Greeks and Egyptians. Most Indian festivals emphasized songs and dances, but the songs were used principally to establish rhythms and the words were of slight importance. Chants were a vital element in most healing ceremonies.

Either the Western Hemisphere received a vital religious stimulus from early voyagers and travelers from distant parts or else the Indian himself by mystical experiences shared a common inspiration with the priestly castes of other nations. The psychologists would probably assume that the esoteric tradition originated in the spiritual needs of the human being, regardless of his race or place of habitation. The search for reality gradually brought into being specialized groups of intensive truth seekers. These groups produced their own leaders, and such wise men and women were acknowledged as divinely inspired, received spontaneous admiration and devotion, were obeyed for their superior endowments, and gradually became a priestly caste. As civilization enlarged the temporal state of the tribe, the religious Societies grew to become powerful institutions, as in Central America. While the tribes remained nomadic, the medicine men were less resplendent and impressive, but their functions were no less significant.

These holy persons seldom took part in war, and frequently were distinguished by a costume combining elements of male and female attire. This practice has been common throughout the religious world and has influenced the dress of pagan priests and Christian clergy alike. The androgynous human being, in whom there is a spiritual union of male and female attributes, has been widely accepted as personifying a supe-

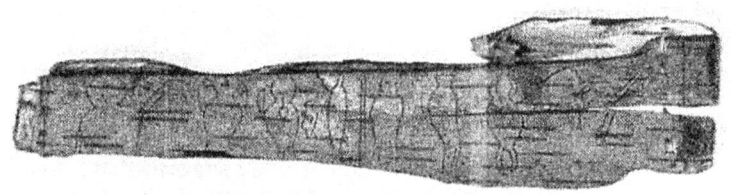

—FROM HOFFMAN'S *THE MIDEWIWIN, ETC.*

Sacred birchbark record of the Mide rituals.

rior type capable of a greater understanding of the Father-wisdom and Mother-love potencies of Divinity. Such symbolism existed in all the great Esoteric Orders of the past.

While ethnologists may be reluctant to admit that the Indians had any formal concept of an esoteric religion, examination into the secret beliefs of the priests of the various tribes shows that they were verging toward the adept tradition, even if it had not matured among them. The Midewiwin, or Great Medicine Society of the Ojibways, initiated both men and women into the secrets of the art of healing and the control of the vital current coursing through the nerve centers of the human body. The Society of the Mides, or shamans, had birchbark rolls which depicted the arrangements of the lodges and included many strange pictographs. Of these, W. J. Hoffman writes: "To persons acquainted with secret societies, a good comparison for the Midewiwin charts would be what is called a trestle board of a Masonic order, which is printed and published and publicly exposed without exhibiting any secrets of the order; yet it is not only significant, but useful to the esoteric in assistance to their memory as to the details of the ceremony."*

The secrets of the Midewiwin were originally communicated to mankind by an initiate-priest, Manabozho, or Great Rabbit, who was a servant of the Good Spirit. The cross was an important symbol in the

*See *7th Annual Report of the Bureau of Ethnology.*

—FROM HOFFMAN'S *THE MIDEWIWIN, ETC.*

General view of the arrangement of the lodge of the Mide.

Midewiwin Rites, and it is interesting that the Mides steadfastly refused to give up their religion and be converted to Christianity.

The controversy as to the possible Masonic significance of the Midewiwin Rites may be noted, but has slight bearing upon the essential facts. Although the birchbark rolls have bestowed prominence upon the activities of this Society, other tribes practiced equally significant rituals and ceremonies. Candidates advanced through four degrees, traveling toward the east, and the lodge rooms were enclosures open to the sky and connecting with each other through doors and passageways. The neophyte was tested and subjected to trials and hazards and also was presented with a sequence of visual arrangements of symbols and other esoteric paraphernalia. The purpose of the Great Medicine Society was to enlighten the human mind and soul and to bind the initiates to the service of their people. It included a method for stimulating extrasensory perceptions and personal investigation into the secrets of Nature.

In 1919, Arthur C. Parker was invited into a secret lodge of the Senecas to witness their ceremonies. Here he heard the legend of Red

Hand, a culture hero, who could hold conversation with the Great Mystery. From the Great Mystery he learned to love all the creatures of the earth, and he spoke the language of the birds and animals. Red Hand was slain by a poisoned arrow because he would not reveal to his assassin the secret of his spiritual power. The animals, discovering by the power of scent that their brother-friend had been killed, gathered in council about his body to find a means of bringing him back to life. Each of the creatures gave part of himself to restore Red Hand to the living. At last the bear came forward, and grasping the hand of the martyred hero raised him by the strong grip of his paw. Those acquainted with the ritual of the Third Degree of the Blue Lodge of Freemasonry will realize that this story must have originated among the rituals of the esoteric schools.

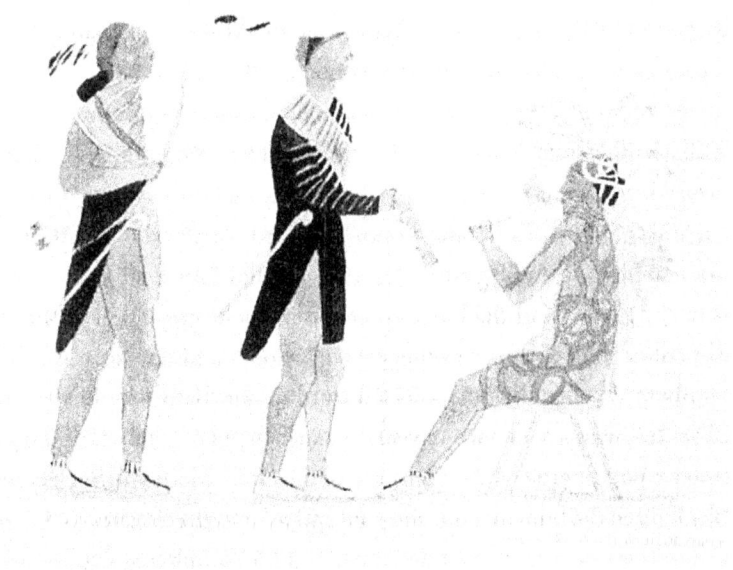

—FROM SCHOOLCRAFT'S *INDIAN TRIBES OF THE UNITED STATES*

Two persons, possibly representing Deganawida and Hiawatha, standing in the presence of Atotharo, the sorcerer-chief of the Iroquois.

Mr. Parker, himself a 32° Mason, sums up the account of his experience in the rites of the Senecas, thus: "Little has been told; the door has only been held ajar the slightest space and no secrets have been revealed. There were feather wands and deerskins, but no purple robes or crowns. Yet, who shall say that the Senecas have not the thread of the legend of Osiris or that they have not an inherent Freemasonry?"*

In the area centering in what is now New York State and extending north and south a considerable distance, the five, later six, nations compromising the Iroquois League attained a high state of social and political integrity. The two great leaders of these Amerinds were Deganawida and Hiawatha. It is impossible to study the life of Deganawida, whose coming was announced by a mysterious visitor from the heaven-world, without realizing that he fulfilled all the requirements of the adept tradition. Deganawida was born of an immaculate conception, possessed the power to work miracles, prayed and fasted, practiced the vigils, was confirmed in his mission by the Great Father, and passed through numerous trials and persecutions. Hiawatha became his first and most distinguished disciple, and these two working together sought to establish everlasting peace among their peoples.

The founder of the Inca dynasty of Peru was the initiate-statesman, Manco Capac, who flourished in the eleventh century A.D. He reformed the social and religious life of the tribes of the Aymara Quichua race. In the capital city of Cuzco which he built, Manco Capac established the religion of the sun. He was a statesman of ability, and claimed to be a direct descendant of the sun god. The empire of the Incas which he founded is remembered especially for its experiments in socialized living. Peru has the distinction of having cradled the first successful Utopia.

Manco Capac emerges as one of the world's outstanding social reformers, with a vision thousands of years ahead of his time. He is said to

*See *American Indian Freemasonry*, by Arthur C. Parker (Buffalo, 1919).

have brought with him to Peru a divine bird in a sacred wicker hamper. This golden falcon is a form of the phoenix, and testifies to the presence of the adept doctrine. Manco Capac combines in his own person the offices of priest and king, like the Melchizedeks of Christian mysticism. Although some historians may be a trifle impulsive when they suggest that Manco Capac was a Buddhist priest, there can be no doubt that the Peruvian culture was heavily influenced by symbols, rituals, and philosophical elements usually associated with the trans-Himalayan area of Central Asia.

In Deganawida, with his Great League, Quetzalcoatl-Kulkulcan and his splendid socialized empires in Mexico and Central America, and Manco Capac and the communal system which he set up in Peru, we have three clear and definite accounts of initiate-leaders establishing schools of esoteric doctrines in the Western Hemisphere. From a consideration of their attainments and the systems which they inaugurated, we can come to but one conclusion: The Mystery Schools of antiquity were represented in the Americas by institutions identical in principle and in purpose with those of Asia and the Mediterranean countries.

Columbus—The Admiral of the Oceans

Prevailing historical accounts which deal with the discovery and colonization of the Western Hemisphere must someday be completely revised. Modern scholars have accepted, without proper reflection, a fabrication of lies fashioned to deceive and to prevent the recognition of facts detrimental, even dangerous, to the ulterior motives of powerful interests. Time will reveal that the continent now known as America was actually discovered and, to a considerable degree, explored more than a thousand years before the beginning of the Christian Era. The true story was in the keeping of the Mystery Schools, and passed from them to the Secret Societies of the medieval world. The Esoteric Orders of Europe,

Asia, and the Near East were in at least irregular communication with the priesthoods of the more advanced Amerindian nations. Plans for the development of the Western Hemisphere were formulated in Alexandria, Mecca, Delhi, and Lhasa long before most European statesmen were aware of the great Utopian program.*

The explorers who opened the New World operated from a master plan and were agents of *re*discovery rather than discoverers. Very little is "known" about the origin, lives, characters, and policies of these intrepid adventurers. Although they lived in a century amply provided with historians and biographers, these saw fit either to remain silent or to invent plausible accounts without substance. Does it not seem remarkable that no one is certain whether Christopher Columbus was actually an English prince, a Greek nobleman, or a Genoese sea captain? Was he granted arms without any examination into his ancestry? Why is it so difficult to ascertain the real name of the man known as Amerigo Vespucci? Who was John Cabot, whose life and exploits are but fragments rather than the sober records of a distinguished citizen? If these men were what they seemed to be, there could have been no advantage gained by such elaborate concealment. If there were a mystery, that which was hidden must have been regarded as valuable.

Plato described the vast continent of Atlantis, which sank beneath the oceans as the result of a seismic cataclysm. There are several possible interpretations of Plato's account. The lost Atlantis could represent a submerged body of knowledge drowned in a sea of forgetfulness. This would explain and justify Bacon's restoration of the fable, which was nothing more than bringing into the light matters long hidden. According to the *Critias,* the oceans became so agitated and laden with mud and slime that navigation to the west ceased. Sailors feared to go beyond the Pillars of Hercules toward those Hesperic Isles sacred to the Mysteries.

---

*See *The Mystery of Columbus,* by Jennings C. Wise.

Even had Christian nations dared to violate the edicts of the Secret Schools, such audacity would have been held in check by the power of Islam, seated in the Holy House at Cairo, and the edicts of Lhasa, backed by the armed strength of the Mongol Empire. The East agreed to preserve the boundaries of Europe, if the European states would bind themselves in a solemn alliance to refrain from exploiting the resources of the Western Hemisphere. Fear of a terrible retribution from beyond the walls of Gog and Magog prevented the Popes from violating their agreement. And without the leadership of the Church, the great families dared not engage in private projects. When the appointed hour came, the Secret Societies selected their own agents to initiate the program of exploration.

"Was Columbus then working," asks Grace A. Fendler, "either as an individual or as a chosen representative of Secret Societies, to bring into expression the old Utopian ideals and to directionalize them across the Seas? Certainly this would go far to explain the charges of 'traitor'; the seizure of all his books and papers; the destruction of all portraiture and likenesses even to the usual mortuary 'busts and arms'; and the complete disappearance of many of his literary works, including the Journal of the First Voyage and the Book of the Second Voyage. All this would then have been mere inquisitional routine, with the rewriting of his biography more or less both of political necessity and a Holy Duty."*

Campanella, in his *Civitas Solis,* causes a Genoese sea captain to be the guest of the Grand Master of the Knights Hospitalers. When Columbus, on the occasion of his first landfall, raised the standard of Castile, he also planted a banner of his own, consisting of a green cross on a white field. Was this a device of the Knights Templar?

The formal education of the man who called himself Christopher

---

*See *New Truths About Columbus.*

Fifteenth-century woodcut representing the landing of Columbus on the island of Hispaniola.

Columbus has been the subject of much speculation. The navigator wrote, in 1501, that during his many voyages to all parts of the world he had met learned men of various races and sects and had "endeavored to see all books of cosmography, history, and philosophy and of other sciences." If the admiral had seriously endeavored to examine early works on navigation, he undoubtedly had noted the references, brief but significant, by Homer, Solon, Aristotle, Pliny, and other ancient authors to "distant lands beyond the great oceans." Plutarch's voyagers must have explored vast areas, and Verplanck Colvin summarizes the old accounts thus: "In the days of Homer, or rather before his time, navigators traveled thousands of miles out into the Atlantic, and back across it . . . they were guided in their voyages by the stars."*

*See *Geographical and Mathematical Discussions of Plutarch's Accounts of Ancient Voyages to the New World.*

One group of "authorities" considers it probable that Columbus was little better than an illiterate sailor, and that his rudiments of learning were derived from a guild school supposed to have been established by the weavers of the city of Genoa. The opposing faction of historians insists that Columbus possessed considerable scholarship even before his celebrated journey. According to Henry Harisse, an outstanding writer on the Columbus mystery, the navigator left ninety-seven manuscripts and over twenty-five thousand marginalia, which may be considered a remarkable achievement for an illiterate. The truth is that the admiral cannot be explained without reference to the Secret Societies, which were the peculiar custodians of the exact information which he required.

The religious and mystical inclinations of the great discoverer are mentioned by most of his biographers. At times Columbus dressed in a plain robe and girdle similar to the costume of the Franciscan Order. It was reported by his son that Columbus died wearing a Franciscan frock. It is not known however, that he was directly associated with this Order, even as a lay Brother. Several religious groups of the times, including Fraternities known to be connected with the esoteric tradition, favored this kind of habit. Perhaps the peculiarities of his costume were overlooked or conveniently forgotten.

The admiral regarded himself as chosen by heaven to fulfill a great mission, and was strengthened by the conviction that he was guarded and guided by the divine providence. Such contemporary reports could imply far more than modern writers would like to acknowledge. In those troublous times, it was customary for the members of Secret Societies to conceal the true source of their instructions by some general statement about heavenly guidance. The mystical instincts of the admiral, his belief in miracles, prophecies, and the doctrine of preordination have been advanced by some critics as proofs of his mental instability.

Referring to what he calls the "colossal, mystical self-confidence" of Columbus, John Bartlet Brebner writes that it was so integral a part of the navigator that "he could believe on one occasion in his voyaging that God had led him to the New Heaven and New Earth of Revelation, and in his darkest hour he knew that God spoke to him in encouragement." On his Third Voyage, the navigator believed that he heard the voice of God speaking words of strength and comfort. On his Fourth Voyage, when great emergencies threatened the entire enterprise, the admiral fell into a trance and a voice spoke to him: "O fool, and slow to believe and to serve thy God, the God of all! What did He do more for Moses, or for David His servant, than He has done for thee?"*

Columbus may have been a disciple or student of the illuminated Raymond Lully. There is a persistent rumor to this effect. He was also involved with the group perpetuating the political convictions of Dante. The following tribute to the Italian poet is indicative and stimulating: "Dante himself was a member of the Albigensian church, and, it is said, for a number of years officiated as pastor of that powerful organization in various European cities. He was a friend of Roger Bacon, and an associate and advisor of powerful leaders in the ancient Order of the Temple, which was at the date of his death, while apparently at the summit of its power, actually nearing its disastrous end. Dante is said to have been an initiate of the esoteric doctrines of the Templars."†

Columbus made use of ciphers and cryptic allegorical expressions and figures of speech. While such ciphers are known to exist in his manuscripts, no systematic effort to decode them has come to public attention. Cecil Jane conjectured that Columbus in his cryptic signatures made use of something resembling a Baconian cipher intended to convey information which could not be directly communicated and to supply the clue to a secret otherwise carefully concealed.‡

Incidentally, the Columbus signature-ciphers are extremely reminis-

---
*See *The Explorers of North America*.
†See *The Montana Mason*, (October, 1921).
‡See *Contemporary Historical Review*, Vol. 1:37.

A fragment of writing in the autograph of Columbus showing his cryptic signature.

cent of the Albigensian papermakers' marks. Seraphim G. Canoutas, J.D., of the University of Athens, in his work *Christopher Columbus, a Greek Nobleman,* attempted to restore the early life of the great discoverer. His findings, calculated to sustain the title of his book, are most illuminating. The secret preparations for the colonizing of the Fortunate Isles, or "the Blessed Isles of the West," were in the keeping of the Albigenses, the Troubadours, and the chivalric Orders of Knighthood. The final phase of the exploration project was left largely to the erudition of Lorenzo the Magnificent and the skill of Leonardo da Vinci. Lorenzo de' Medici was a distinguished Platonist, a patron of Secret Societies, the founder of an important philosophical school, and a subtle adversary of the Borgias. Leonardo was a faithful agent of the great Florentine prince, and one of those men possessed by the spirit of "towardness." Although Lorenzo did not live to see the fulfillment of the Great Plan, he spoke the magic word which opened for Columbus the most exclusive institutions in Europe and invested him with the temporal means for acquiring a measure of consideration from liberal princes and scholars. It was the invisible hand of the Medici that balanced on end the celebrated egg.

The conclusions of Columbus concerning the shape of the earth indicate that he was acquainted with the esoteric traditions of Asia and the

—PORTRAIT BY VASARI
Lorenzo De' Medici, called the Magnificent.

Near East. He partly revealed the source of his own instructions when he declared the planet to be shaped like a pear, the upper end of which projected toward the sky, like the boss in the center of a shield. The top of this protuberance was the terrestrial paradise, where none could go except by the grace of God. The admiral noted that this shape coincided with the opinions of certain holy and wise theologians, but he failed to mention the sects or religions to which they belonged. The earth-mountain was certainly the Meru of the Brahmans and the sacred hill of the Egyptian Mysteries. Mount Meru, like Chang Shambhala, Olympus, and the peak described in The Revelation are all veiled allusions to the Invisible Government of the earth.

Nor should it be assumed that all historical uncertainties centered around Christopher Colon, the dove of Genoa. The case of John Cabot is equally curious. There may be more than passing interest in the observations of one research student: "When Columbus, in the interim between voyages disappears from public view, John Cabot appears and permanently disappears when Columbus reappears."* It is easy to forget that John Cabot was really Giovanni Caboto, born in Genoa and a naturalized citizen of Venice. It was especially mentioned that in one of his journeys Cabot visited Mecca, and, like Columbus, was acquainted with the wise men of the Near East. It has even been suggested that he had contacted the religious and political convictions of the secret Christian sect of the Johannites, which played so large a part in the esoteric doctrines of the Templars.

Cabot conveniently found the ear of the English king, and was immediately entrusted with a delicate diplomatic mission to Denmark to arbitrate disputes over the fisheries of Iceland. Grace Fendler also notes that the records of the English Privy Purse shows a pension paid to one Antonio Cabot for several years after John Cabot was historically dead. The pension passed through the hands of an English merchant named Rici D'Americke. The voyages of Cabot were important inasmuch as they resulted in a division which gave most of North America to the English group which was free from the theological and mercenary pressures of the Spanish program.

The Great Plan reached the Western Hemisphere through a series of incidents. Many early explorers and colonizers are known to have been associated with Secret Societies. There is no historical way of determining the secret spiritual convictions of so-called conquistadors, adventurers, and founders of plantations. It is a well-established fact that arts, sciences, philosophies, and political convictions accompany less valuable merchandise along trade routes and caravan trails. Some of the colonizers were probably unaware of the parts they were playing, and the settlements which they founded remained for generations with-

---

*See *New Truths About Columbus*, by Grace A. Fendler.

out the strength or security to advance ideological programs. The work, then as always, was in the hands and keeping of a few initiated leaders. They were responsible for the results, and they built slowly and wisely, thinking not of their own days or of their own reputation, but of the future in which the Great Plan would be fulfilled.

The Colonization Scheme

The political intrigues which Queen Elizabeth had inherited from Henry VIII plagued Her Majesty's advisors throughout her long reign. Henry had rebelled against the papacy, ousted its clergy, closed its monastic houses, confiscated its properties, and established the Church of England. Spain, motivated by both religious and secular considerations, was resolved to control England. The Spanish ambassador at the court of the Tudors was the moving spirit behind an elaborate program of espionage, and all that he could learn, glean, or deduce was dispatched posthaste to his royal master, the king of Spain.

While serving his diplomatic apprenticeship at the court of Navarre, Bacon had been initiated into the new liberalism represented throughout Europe by Secret Societies of intellectuals dedicated to civil and religious freedom. He returned to England fully aware of the intentions of Philip II, the Spanish king. Later, when the moment was propitious, he threw the weight of his literary group with the English colonization plan for America in order to prevent Spanish dominations of the New World. The same political considerations apparently also induced him to develop Freemasonry as a further bulwark against the encroachments of the Spanish plot. Cherishing as he did the dream of a great commonwealth in the New Atlantis, Bacon was resolved to prevent his plan from being frustrated by a dominant clergy, supporting and supported by an entrenched aristocracy.

It was necessary for Bacon to conceal both his purposes and the machinery for their fulfillment from the Spanish spies. If the project were prematurely revealed, it could precipitate a desperate political situation. With many courtiers secretly sympathizing with the cause of Spain, and Elizabeth's claim to the throne questioned because of Henry's numerous divorces, it was impossible to use such conventional channels as were provided by an uneasy government. Bacon protected both his cause and his country by acting privately and maturing his schemes within the hallowed walls of the Inns of Court. There in the sanctuary of the martyred Templars, who had earlier felt the full weight of ecclesiastical displeasure, he labored industriously to fashion wings for the White Horse of Britain.

The rapid progress of England in the second half of the sixteenth and the first half of the seventeenth centuries was due not only to the appearance of a select coterie of wits, but also to the more liberal atmosphere which resulted from "Harry's" religious housecleaning. After the Armada, the issues were partly clarified, but it still remained vital to protect and enlarge the English interests in the Western Hemisphere. Incidentally, the ships of the Armada carried ninety Spanish Inquisitors, with all the paraphernalia of their office, ready to set up the Inquisition in conquered England. The Pope had already claimed the three Americas for the Church, but the English colonizers were resolved to dispute this claim with every resource at their disposal.

The first permanent English settlement in North America was established at Jamestown, Virginia, on May 14, 1607. Earlier attempts resulted only in the naming of the region, which was called Virginia in honor of Queen Elizabeth. In 1609, Sir George Somers was appointed governor of the colony of Virginia. He sailed for the New World with dignity appropriate to his office, but his arrival was delayed when his ship foundered on the Hog Islands. Later he was able to victual two pinnaces with prime pork and to proceed on his journey. The Hog Islands, so named because of the wild swine that infested them, were renamed the Somers Islands in honor of Sir George's impromptu visit. Ultimately, however, these islands were called the Bermudas, after the Spanish navigator Juan Bermudez.

The Somers Islands shilling.

In 1609, James I granted a charter to the Bermuda Company, and in 1612, Richard More and sixty colonists from Virginia settled on one of the islands. Later, in 1616, Captain John Smith appointed Master Daniel Tucker as governor of Bermuda. The same year, a series of coins was struck off for use in the Bermudas. The history of this coinage is extremely obscure. The Hog Money, as it is often called, was of brass and in three denominations. The shilling of this issue bears on the obverse the legend "Sommer Islands," surrounding the figure of a wild boar. Above the boar is the numeral XII, signifying twelvepence. There is no date. The reverse of the coin is a ship under full sail. The wild boar on this coinage carries the definite impression of being a heraldic device. It is identical in drawing with the crest of Lord Bacon, even to the jaunty curl of its porcine tail.

According to the meager records in the British Museum, this coinage was forbidden by James I to be exported. It seems strange that the Hog Money should have been regarded so unfavorably by the king. Why did James on two separate occasions act so strenuously to prevent the circulation of this coinage? The *Encyclopaedia Britannica* (1946) intimates that the coins were struck in America, but numismatic catalogues describe them as made *for* America. From the evidence of the coins themselves, it would seem that the Hog Money was a definite landmark, bearing witness to the operations of the Secret Society directing the early colonization program.

The adventures of Sir George Somers were quickly adapted to high drama by the literary workshop at Gray's Inn. The most obvious example of their ingenuity was *The Tempest*. This play first appeared about one and a half years after the governor had been shipwrecked. According to the chronological chart of the Shakespearean plays, *The Tempest* was first acted in 1611, was played a second time in 1613, but was not published until the great folio of 1623. It is supposed that the play was written between 1608 and 1610, but there is no data as to whether or not it was among those rewritten before final publication.

The character of Prospero, magician, philosopher, and Duke of Milan, is believed to be based upon a historical person whose name was Prospero Colonna. It is interesting that Columbus usually signed himself "Colon," and that Lord Baron has been referred to as "the little Columbus of literature." *The Tempest* also introduces an "honest old counselor," by name Gonzalo, who seems dedicated to a utopian mood. He refers to the magic isle as a "commonwealth," and explains that if he had a plantation there (a term used in describing colonial grants in America) he would design it along communal lines, concluding:

> All things in common Nature should produce
> Without sweat or endeavor: treason, felony,
> Sword, pike, knife, gun, or need of any engine
> Would I not have: but Nature should bring forth
> Of its own kind, all foyzon, all abundance
> To feed my innocent people.

The patrons of the Virginia Company included Lord Southampton and those two, that "incomparable paire," William, Earl of Pembroke, and Philip, Earl of Montgomery, to whom the first folio of Shakespeare was dedicated. These excellent gentlemen also permitted the use of their names as patrons of that company of actors which included William Shakespeare—a tight little corporation, to say the least. So elaborate a plan would not have been necessary had the colonization program involved nothing more than the granting of land to royal favorites.

It makes little practical difference whether the flora and fauna of *The Tempest* resembles the Bermudas, or as Dr. Hale suggests, corresponds more closely with the Cuttyhunk Island off the coast of Massachusetts. The opponents of the Bermudian hypothesis insist that the play would have mentioned the wild hogs had these islands been the locale of the story. If Bacon and his Society were involved in the project, it would scarcely have been advisable for them to emphasize the hog symbol, which had already been used with discretion on several occasions. They could not afford to tie the Shakespearean productions so obviously with their scheme. They were satisfied to leave their mark and seal on the emblematic coinage.

The "brave New World," referred to by Miranda, is certainly America and not some insignificant island. Prospero is the magician of the New Age, the exponent of the Baconian "method." He binds the elements to his service, and the story of his adventures is an improvisation upon the grand theme of the Utopias. It was also in this "brave New World" that he buried his magic staff and drowned his book; that is, concealed in appropriate places the formulas which were the secret of his power.

Thomas Jefferson examined the "repositories" of the Bacon group in colonial America, checked their contents, and caused them to be resealed for future ages. Several attempts have been made to locate these "philosophical tombs," including excavations in England, Newfoundland, and Virginia. What is believed to be an important Baconian vault was located, with the help of coded tombstones, in Williamsburg, Virginia, in 1938.*

After his "banishment" from public life, Bacon muses thus upon the philosophical advantages of political decline: "Methinks they are resembled by those of Sir George Somers, who being bound by his employment to another coast, was by *tempest* cast upon the Bermudas. And therefore a ship wrack'd man made full discovery of a new temperate fruitful region, which none had before inhabited; and which Mariners, who had only seen its rocks, had esteemed an inaccessible and enchanted place." In his advice to Sir George Villiers, Bacon expressed the same sentiments which had been incorporated in the Broadsides of the Council for Virginia. According to Alexander Brown, "he may have taken these ideas from those Broadsides, or he may have been one of the original authors of them, as he was a member of that Council."†

The same author was so impressed by Bacon's references to "tempest and the inaccessible and enchanted Bermudas" that he asks: "May not Bacon have aided Shakespeare in compiling *some* of his plays? . . . Bacon always had a fancy for such things." Dr. Brown also mentions the Bacon family in America, noting that Benjamin Harrison, the twenty-third president of the United States, was *doubly* descended from this family.

It is not without reason that Lord Bacon, who has been called "the moving spirit in the colonization scheme," included Christopher Columbus as one of the "great inventors."‡ Judge Brown writes of Bacon's participation in the settlement of Newfoundland: "It was entirely due to the Great Chancellor's influence that the king granted the ad-

---
*See *Foundations Unearthed*, by Marie Bauer.
†See *Genesis of the United States*.
‡See *The New Atlantis*.

STAMP OF NEWFOUNDLAND
Issued to commemorate the tercentenary of the colonization scheme and Lord Bacon, its guiding spirit.

vances and issued the Charters to Bacon and his associates in Guy's Newfoundland Company."* *The Colonial State Calendar* contains the following extract of patent: "To Henry, Earl of Northampton, Sir Francis Bacon, and others, for the Colony or plantation in Newfoundland from 46° to 52° N. Lat., together with the seas and islands lying within ten leagues of the coast." The same notes: "A letter is mentioned from John Smith to Lord Bacon enclosing description of New England, the extraordinary profits arising from the *fisheries,* and great facilities for *plantation.*"

William Hepworth Dixon, of the Inner Temple, writing in 1861, makes several important observations concerning the settlement of the New World. A few fragments will indicate the direction of his thinking: "In no History of America, in no Life of Bacon, have I found one word to connect him with the plantation of that great Republic. Yet, like Raleigh and Delaware, he takes an active share in the labours, a conspicuous part in the sacrifices through which the foundations of Virginia and the Carolinas are first laid. Like men of far less note, who have received far

---

*See *History of Newfoundland.*

higher honours in America, Bacon pays his money into the great Company, and takes office in its management as one of the Council. To his other glories therefore must be added that of a Founder of New States. . . .

"All generous spirits rush to the defense of Virginia. Bacon joins the Company with purse and voice. Montgomery, Pembroke, and Southampton, the noble friends of Shakespeare, join it. . . . A fleet, commanded by Gates and Somers, sails from the Thames, to meet on its voyage at sea those singular and poetic storms and trials which add the Bermudas to our empire and *The Tempest* to our literature. . . .

"One hundred and seventy-five years after Walter Raleigh laid down his life in Palace Yard for America, his illustrious blood paid for by Gondomar in Spanish gold, the citizens of Carolina, framing for themselves a free constitution, remembered the man to whose genius they owed their existence as a state. They called the capital of their country *Raleigh*. The United States can also claim among their muster roll of Founders the no less noble name of Francis Bacon. Will the day come, when, dropping such feeble names as Troy and Syracuse, the people of the Great Republic will give the august and immortal name of Bacon to one of their splendid cities?"*

Sir Walter Raleigh, a distinguished member of the Baconian circle, made the mistake of confiding his private plans for his South American expedition to the king. James promised to keep the secret with his honor, but hastened to whisper it in the ear of Count Gondomar. The Spanish, property forewarned, had a strong force waiting for Raleigh at the mouth of the Orinoko, and in the fighting that followed, Raleigh's son was killed. James, who was to blame for the whole sorry business, promised Gondomar that Raleigh would be publicly executed, but even the popular account of the knight's death is false. Under such conditions, it would have been madness to preserve the papers of any significant political

---

*See *Personal History of Lord Bacon.*

SIR WALTER RALEIGH
Portrait in the first edition of his great folio volume *The History of the World*.

project. That which was intentionally concealed, even from the records of state, cannot easily be recovered after so long a time. It was an axiom of that day that a wise man was like a trunk with a double bottom—when first opened, the trunk must seem to be empty. Only those of kindred spirit could know that a man's character had a secret compartment.

James Spedding, an outstanding authority on Bacon's life, writes: "We learn incidentally from one of Bacon's apopthegyms that soon after he became Lord Keeper (which would be shortly before Raleigh sailed), he had a long conversation with him in Gray's Inn walks. We are not told what the subject was, but it must have been interesting, and was probably important, for it was then that he kept the Earl of Exeter so long waiting upstairs."*

Benjamin Disraeli gave some attention to that extraordinary volume, *The History of the World*, which Sir Walter Raleigh is supposed to have written during his confinement in the Tower of London. Disraeli, whose scholarship equipped him to weigh the difficulties of so vast a project, concluded that Raleigh, whose natural inclinations and opportunities belied the work, must have received considerable assistance from other wits. He listed several candidates for the honors of coauthorship, but if Disraeli stated the dilemma skillfully, his solutions are inconclusive. The only names of interest which he advanced were the Earl of Northumberland and Ben Jonson.†

Bacon visited Raleigh during his imprisonment, and the friendship between the two men was sufficiently founded upon previous efforts which Bacon had made to cement a genuine alliance between Raleigh and the unfortunate Earl of Essex. Ben Jonson acted as intermediary and agent extraordinary on several occasions. It will be remembered that Jonson was at Stratford on that festive evening which is said to have contributed to the "Bard's" demise. If Shakespeare had small Latin and less Greek, it is unlikely that Raleigh had more Hebrew. The first edition of *The History of the World* is embellished with numerous emblems and devices belonging to the Baconian group. The title page has been a subject of controversy for centuries. Ben Jonson, referring to Sir Walter Raleigh, told Drummond: "The best wits in England were employed in making his history."

Bacon became a member of the Virginia Company in 1609. The charters of that year and of 1612, drafted by Sandys, were prepared for

---

*See *The Life and Times of Francis Bacon*.
†See *Curiosities of Literature*.

the king's signature by Sir Henry Hobart and Sir Francis Bacon. To Bacon's interest in the colonies, testimony is borne by William Strachey in the dedication (dated 1618) of a manuscript copy of his *Historie of Travaile into Virginia Britania*: "Your Lordship ever approaving yourself a most noble fautor (favorer) of the Virginia plantation, being from the beginning (with other lords and earles) of the principal counsell applyed to propagate and guide yt." One of the reasons why there is so much difficulty in tracing Bacon's activities in connection with the plantation is that the records of the Privy Council to the year 1613 were destroyed by fire at Whitehall in 1618. Incidentally, the boundaries of the original Virginia Colony extended to the west coast of California.

Charles Mills Gayley divides the group instrumental in the foundation of the Virginia Company of London into two sections: the Liberals, or patriots, and the Imperialists, who supported the king in reserving to the Crown the right to form the government of the colonies and plantations. This conflict was the real source of the Revolution of 1775, which resulted in the complete independence of the American colonies. Among the Liberals, Gayley includes Christopher Brooke and John Seldon. "They were both, in their hours of ease, poets after a fashion, members of the pastoral coterie of the Inns of Court. . . . Brooke's bosom friend was the poet Donne. He was also intimate with Shakespeare's follow dramatists, Jonson and Drayton, and his epic dramatic admirer, Davies of Hereford."

Gayley shows the usual systematic indifference to Bacon's part in the colonization plan, and the few references which he makes to his lordship are consistently derogatory. He does, however, mention that Bacon, in his essay "Of Plantation," which was not published until after the great chancellor's death, appeared to agree with the practical phase of the Liberals' policy. Gayley says: "Bacon may have collaborated with Sandys, but his interest in the colonies was romantic and always for the glorification of the Crown."

In a speech given at Gray's Inn Hall, an American, the Honorable James Beck, remarked that the two charters of government, which were the beginning of constitutionalism in America and therefore the germ of the Constitution of the United States, were drawn up by Lord Bacon. He added that Bacon, "the immortal treasurer of Gray's Inn," visioned the future and predicted the growth of America in the memorable words: "This Kingdom now first in His Majesty's time hath gotten a lot or portion in the New World by the plantation of Virginia and the Summer Islands. And certainly it is with the Kingdom of the Earth as it is in the Kingdom of Heaven, sometimes a grain of mustard seed proves a great tree."*

In a speech touching the recovering of "drowned mineral works," prepared for the Parliament by the Viscount of St. Albans, the Lord High Chancellor of England indicated his intention of making an immediate and practical application of his philosophical theory. Bacon's words should be carefully studied, for here is a remarkable example of double meaning. He says: "For, by this unchangeable way (my Lords) have I proposed to erect the Academical Fabric of the Island's *Salomon's House,* modelled in my *New Atlantis.* And I can hope (my Lords) that my Midnight Studies to make our Countries flourish and outvy *European* Neighbors in mysterious and beneficent Arts, have not so ingratefully affected the whole Intellects, that you will delay or resist his Majesty's desires, and my humble Petition in this Benevolent, yea, Magnificent Affair; Since your Honourable Posterities may be enriched thereby, and my Ends are only, to make the World my Heir, and the learned Fathers of my *Salomon's House,* the successive and sworn Trustees in the dispensation of this great Service, for God's Glory, my Prince's Magnificence, this Parliaments Honour, our Countries general Good, and the propagation of my own Memory. . . . Which done, I shall not then doubt the happy

*See *American Baconiana,* Feb. 19, 1923.

—FROM CASE'S *SPHAERA CIVITATIS*

Queen Elizabeth as the presiding genius of the sphere of moral virtues.

Issue of my Undertakings in this Design, whereby concealed Treasures, which now seem utterly lost to Mankind, shall be confined to so universal a Piety, and brought into use by the industry of Converted Penitents."*

For "Midnight Studies," works in darkness or secret projects should be read. The "sworn Trustees" were, of course, the members of his eso-

---

Baconiana, or Certain Genuine Remains of Sr. Francis Bacon, etc. (London, 1679)

teric group. The "concealed Treasures" were his discoveries toward truth, and the "Converted Penitents" were those not initiated into the mysteries, although it is usual to assume that they were convicts exported to work in the plantation.

Until the formation of the Virginia Company, the Jamestown settlement was a tragic example of shortsightedness and mismanagement. The colonizers were drawn principally from the genteel classes and were totally unequipped to carve out their destinies in the wilderness. Among the early arrivals were jewelers and a perfumer. Several were fortune hunters, and all would have come to a bad end had not Captain John Smith been a rough-and-ready soldier, whose exploits included warfare against the Turks in Transylvania. Among these assorted "gentles," however, there were some with capacities suitable for the transference to the Western Hemisphere of the projects designed by the wits of Gray's Inn.

After the Jamestown settlement gained some semblance of order and permanence, descendents of those men who formed the original Baconian Society left England and settled in the colony. It was through them that the Great Plan began to operate in America. There were most fortuitous marriages between the families of the original custodians of the philosophical legacy. From the minglings of the bloods of the Bacons, the Wottons, the Donnes, the Herberts, and the Mores, the Virginia colony derived many of its prominent citizens. Lord Bacon guided the project and probably outlined the program to be followed after his death.

The Reverend M. F. Carey, associate of the Philosophical Society of Great Britain, writes: "We are furnished with no documentary evidence of the introduction of Freemasonry into the United States; but it appears that it had an existence there as early as the year 1606."* Charles H. Merz supports the belief that certain "Masonic" activities must be assigned to the period between 1600 and 1620. He writes: "There is

*See *Freemasonry in All Ages*.

much to indicate that the period of Bacon was the beginning of a secret 'floor work,' an idea that afterwards, imperfectly understood, was welded to the Operative or Guild System and became the curious Anderson and Desaguliers mixture of 1723.... Someone must have drawn freely from such works as Utopia, Atlantis, Campanella, Shakespeare, the Bible and other sources for the curious conglomeration of Rosicrucian, Religious, Mystic and Operative laws, rules and government that our ritual presents."*

The Bacon family itself was well represented in Virginia, both by name and by blood. It has been usual to trace the Bacons of Virginia from Robert Bacon of Drinkstone, Suffolk, who was the father of the good Sir Nicholas Bacon, Lord Keeper of the Great Seal. Sir Nicholas' brother, James Bacon, had a son, Sir James Bacon, who died in 1618. Sir James was the father of Nathaniel Bacon (the elder), whose grandson was Nathaniel Bacon, the rebel, who led the Bacon Rebellion in Virginia. Nathaniel, the elder, had a brother, the Reverend James Bacon, whose son, also named Nathaniel Bacon, came to Virginia in 1650 and settled at King's Creek in York County. This Nathaniel was a sober and thoughtful man who concerned himself considerably in the affairs of his "uneasy cousin," Nathaniel, the rebel. Both of the Nathaniels have been referred to by historians as Lord Bacon's "kinsmen." The private records do not agree entirely with the accepted genealogy, but this supplies enough material to demonstrate the natural and available channels for the transference of Lord Bacon's projects and remains to Virginia.

Nathaniel, the rebel (1647-1676), graduated at Cambridge and studied law at the Inns of Court. He married in 1674, and sailed for Virginia the same year. He had ample financial resources, secured several estates, was socially prominent, and was appointed to the Governor's Council. When Governor Berkeley refused to protect the colonists from

---

*See *Guild Masony in the Making*.

the neighboring Indian tribes, young Bacon took the field in defiance of the governor's pleasure. A feud approaching revolution resulted, which ended by Nathaniel Bacon and his followers burning the Jamestown settlement. The episode is referred to historically as Bacon's Rebellion, and it has been said that the occurrence played an important part in the formation of the American national consciousness. Bacon's career as a rebel lasted about twenty weeks, and he is supposed to have died of poison or malaria, October 1, 1676, while campaigning. The circumstances of his death are obscure, and his body was buried in an unmarked grave to prevent Governor Berkeley from ordering the corpse to be dug up and publicly hanged. There is more to this story than has ever been told.

Bacon's Rebellion took place exactly one hundred years before the colonies of America declared themselves to be a free and independent nation in 1776. The causes of the Rebellion and the Revolution were similar, if not identical. In 1676, Bacon, the rebel, said: "But if there be (as sure there is) a just God to appeal to, if religion and justice be a sanctuary here, if to plead the cause of the oppressed, if sincerely to aim at his Majesty's honour, and the public good without any reservation or by-interest, if to stand in the gap after so much blood of our dear brethren bought and sold, if after the loss of a great part of his Majesty's colony deserted and dispeopled freely with our lives and estates to save the remainder, be reason—God Almighty judge and let guilty die."*

Although Bacon, the rebel, was certainly an impetuous young man, his cause was just and his sentiments precisely those of his "noble kinsman." Governor Berkeley represented the same entrenched tyranny against which the Universal Reformation had been fashioned and perfected. In justice, however, it should be noted that Berkeley was summoned to England to explain his conduct. The king refused him audience and is credited with saying: "That old fool has hanged more

*See *Old Virginia and Her Neighbours*, by John Fiske.

men in that naked country than I have done for the murder of my father." Berkeley died the following year—of vexation.

As settlements by the Spanish, Dutch, French, and English increased in number and size, no political, philosophical, or mystical sect of Western Europe was without members or sympathizers among the colonizers. Europe was aflame with new ideals affecting every department of human activity. Old World theories became New World practices. Reactionaries and progressives arrived together, but found no substantial reconciliation. Nonconformists continued to be persecuted, and found it necessary to seek refuge in the wilderness or among friendly Indian tribes. Little has been made of these dissentions, and the dissenters themselves have been traditionally regarded as troublesome.

It is difficult to restore the pattern of submerged activities covering a period when historical records were scanty and subject to destruction. It is certain, however, that between 1610 and 1660 a mass of material concerned with the development of the Great Plan for America was transferred from Europe to the Western Continent for preservation and future use. It is shallow thinking to assume that the Secret Societies operating in Europe—the Freemasons, the Rosicrucians, and the Fellows of the Royal Society—had no representation among the colonies until the beginning of the eighteenth century. The confusion is due not to the lack of such activity, but to the inadequacy of available records.

Reverend Edward Patterson, in his *History of Rhode Island* (page 101) refers to a Masonic document found in America which says: "In the spring of 1658, Mordecai Campaunall, Moses Packeckoe, Levi, and others, in all fifteen families, arrived at New Port (America), from Holland. They brought with them the first three degrees of Masonry, and worked them in the house of Campaunall, and continued to do so, they and their successors, to the year 1742."

Johannes Kelpius and the Pietists of Pennsylvania

It has been claimed that the Rosicrucians and possibly other initiate Orders of Europe established themselves in the American colonies during the closing years of the seventeenth century. The best-publicized candidate for the honor of having brought the Esoteric Schools to the New World was the German theological student and mystical Pietist, Magister Johannes Kelpius. It is believed that Kelpius was initiated into the mysteries of cabalistic philosophy during his university days by the celebrated esotericist, Christian Knorr, Baron von Rosenroth. This learned man edited and translated numerous works relating to obscure subjects, and is especially remembered for his *Kabbala Denudata*. He was a mystic, and published a collection of hymns under the stimulating title *Neuer Helicon mit Seiner Neun Musen, etc.*

Kelpius lived for some years as an anchorite in a cave in what is now Fairmount Park, Philadelphia, and died in 1708 as the result of exposure and extreme austerities. The direct cause of his death was tuberculosis. John Kelpius came of a substantial family of Siebenburgen. He was educated in the University of Helmstadt, and regarded Dr. Fabricius, professor of theology at Helmstadt, with special esteem. In a letter addressed to Dr. Fabricius, Kelpius opens with the salutation "Your Magnificence." On February 7, 1694, Kelpius charted the ship *Sarah Maria,* of which Captain John Tanner, an Englishman, was the master, for the sum of seven pounds, and with his small band of German Pietists began the long and dangerous journey to Pennsylvania. They reached their destination after numerous hardships about ten weeks later.

Kelpius was twenty-three years old when he arrived at Germantown. Finding this bustling community too worldly, the group retired into the depths of the lower Wissahickon woods, where they built a hermitage. Here they formed themselves into the Society of the Woman of

—FROM SACHSE'S *THE GERMAN PIETISTS OF PROVINCIAL PENNSYLVANIA*
The only known likeness of the Magister, from the original painting by Dr. Christopher Witt now in the Historical Society of Pennsylvania.

the Wilderness, where they consecrated their efforts toward spiritual preparations for the millennium. The brethren became known as the Hermits of the Ridge, and combined their spiritual ministrations with horoscopy, magic, divination, and healing. Kelpius is credited with laying out the first botanical garden in America. He died sitting in a chair in his garden, surrounded by his sorrowing disciples, in the thirty-fifth year of his life. He was buried in the area, but the location of the grave is not known. His community passed with him, although a few of his celibate followers survived him by many years. Most of the group joined the Mennonite community at Ephrata, and others returned to the simple religious life of the Germantown citizens. The little sect of solitudinarians left little more than a gentle, but eccentric, tradition in the New World. In the library of the Francke Institutions at Halle, in Saxony, there is a manuscript in the autograph of Pastor Heinrich Muhlenberg which describes the death of Kelpius. Feeling that his end was near, the Magister called in his trusted friend, Daniel Geissler. He handed Geissler a small chest or casket securely sealed, and told him to cast it into the Schuylkill River in a place where the water was deep. Geissler carried the curious box to the riverbank and decided to hide it there until after the Magister's death. When he returned to the bedside of the dying Kelpius, the Master raised himself on his elbow and rebuked Geissler for disobeying his instructions and concealing the casket. Geissler, convinced that Kelpius had strange powers of second sight, went back and threw the small chest into the water. As it fell into the stream, the sealed box exploded, and for some time flashes of lightning and great roaring sounds came out of the river.

Kelpius, writing in 1699, explained the origin and doctrines of his Order. The Pietists were conscientious objectors to the corruptions existing in organized theologies. Their reforms were accompanied by ecstasies, revelations, inspirations, illuminations, inspeakings, prophecies, apparitions, changing of minds, transfigurations, translations of bodies, fastings, paradisiacal representations of voices, melodies, and sensations. It is difficult to conceive that the Rosicrucians, as they were known through their original documents, would lay claim to such procedures.

Pietism, a seventeenth-century mystical sect, arose modestly in Frankfurt as a spiritual revolt against the intellectual orthodoxy of German Protestantism. It spread moderately, and the members gained inspiration and comfort from the mystical teachings of Jakob Boehme. Its principal leaders were Philip Jakob Spener and August Hermann Francke. It was Spener who instituted the famous *Collegia Pietatis,* a kind of meeting of minds for the study of sacred matters. Francke, a Hebrew and Greek scholar, was learned, virtuous, and industrious and much admired in the community where he resided.

The Pietists held many Puritan convictions, indulged millenarian speculations, and dabbled in mystical arts, and their approach to religious matters is said to have most resembled the devotional concepts of the early Franciscans. The principal emphasis was upon religious experience as the direct means of attaining Christian insight. The Moravians are considered a direct offshoot of Pietism, as to a degree was the Methodist revival under John Wesley.

Although the Pietist communities in Pennsylvania were given to mystical speculation, even to a little cabalism and folk magic, few genuine Rosicrucian landmarks have been discovered among their remains. They were religious enthusiasts, and the inner circle was so devout in its practice of continence that it became extinct within fifty years. Magister Kelpius seems to have studied astrology and the metaphysics of Jakob Boehme, and relics relating to these subjects are scattered about the valley of Ephrata. Some of the Pietists gave thought to alchemy, attempted the calculation of the millennium, located water with the divining rod, and wore magical amulets and talismans. They were Second Adventists, and a few believed that they would be translated bodily into the spiritual world without suffering physical death.

Dr. Julius Friedrich Sachse was the principal historian of the Germantown communities which flourished in and about Lancaster County, Pennsylvania, during the eighteenth and early nineteenth centuries. In his books *The German Pietists of Provincial Pennsylvania* (Philadelphia, 1895) and *The Diarium of Magister Johannes Kelpius* (Lancaster, 1917) he attempted to prove that the Kelpius brethren were Rosicrucians. As the original Pietists never claimed such an association, Dr. Sachse based his conclusions upon circumstantial evidence. He advanced seals, signets, ornate symbolic crosses, fragments of mystical rituals, and certain books and manuscripts discovered in the area to support his opinions. These relics, though indicating a devotion to metaphysical speculation, are not sufficiently Rosicrucian in themselves to justify their acceptance as prima-facie evidence.

Some of these religious curiosities may be authentic productions of the Society or its members, but until it is determined how and when they were brought to the New World and by what authority it is unwise to jump to conclusions. Many of the immigrants brought with them all of their worldly goods, and we cannot assume that a man belonged to a Secret Society merely because one or two books dealing with the Society, and available to anyone, were found among his effects.

Through the courtesy of the daughter of the late Dr. Sachse, it has been possible to examine the Rosicrucian manuscript formerly belonging to him and some other German mystical books which he regarded as indicating Rosicrucian influence. Zimmerman, the astronomer who predicted the end of the world in 1694, was a close friend of Kelpius. Certainly the prophecy was a failure, and it scarcely seems reasonable that the Rosicrucian Brotherhood should move to Pennsylvania, via the good ship *Sarah Maria,* and there organize themselves out of existence by the extremeness of their vows and religious obligations.

On the other hand, it is quite possible that Kelpius was a member of one of the semisecret Adventist movements which had strong followings in Germany and the Low Countries. His manner of life indicates that he was bound by religious obligations, and bound others to himself and the cause which he represented by similar vows. He did not, however, fulfill the requirements set forth in the Manifestoes of the Rosy Cross, which insisted that members of the Society remain inconspicuous by refraining from any public practices that might draw attention to themselves.

Because almost nothing is actually known about the mystical convictions of the Kelpians, their part in the transference of esoteric lore from Europe to America has been considerably exaggerated. There is nothing whatever to prove that as a sect they were more than they appeared to be, and they laid down most impermanent footings. Individual members probably were acquainted with the reformation projected by Secret Societies on the Continent and in England, but these signs and portents were interpreted as foreshadowing the approaching millennium. The Pietists could scarcely have been devoted Second Adventists had they any vision of an extensive program for the building of a new social order in the Western Hemisphere, nor did their activities imply any plan for the future or any program for the expansion of the philosophical or mystical aspects of their belief. There is not even the suggestion that Kelpius selected a successor or had any intention of transferring any authority, spiritual or temporal.

Among the unusual religious groups that settled in Pennsylvania were the Mennonites, the Labadists, the Dunkers, the Neugeborenen, the Schwenkfelders, and the Moravian brethren. Most of these sects held convictions that could be interpreted as mystical. In all probability, however, the Rosicrucian descent was established considerably earlier by the English colonials of Virginia. The mystics of the Wissahickon, according to the actual words of Kelpius, shared the convictions and perpetuated the doctrines of the Quietists and Chiliasts, who struggled for existence among the Protestant communities of Germany and Switzerland.

The Pietists were channels through which books on cabalism, alchemy, astrology, and the Hermetic arts reached the New World. Thus, they contributed to the westward motion of the Philosophic Empire. Their own practices, however, detracted seriously from their usefulness as reformers or educators, and their influence was limited to the neighborhood wherein they dwelt. Kelpius was a devout man, possibly well-learned, but most of his followers were more earnest than informed, and there seems to have been no vision among them of a broad or enduring ministry. This Order of the Mustard Seed never fulfilled the promise of the parable. It not only failed to increase, but also perished in the foreign soil.

The American Revolutionary Period

No study of the descent of the adept tradition through the Baconian group would be complete without reference to *The Life and Adventures of Common Sense,* which was published in 1769 and was described as "an Historical Allegory." The work appeared anonymously, but is attributed on slight evidence to Herbert Lawrence, a surgeon and apothecary and an intimate friend of David Garrick. This book was the first to attribute the authorship of the Shakespeare plays to Sir Francis Bacon, but that reference, while the best-known, is not by any means the most important fragment of the text. Bacon seems to appear personified under the pseudonym "Wisdom." His lordship's departure to Holland is specifically mentioned, and the descent of the Great Plan is traced allegorically from the schools of Greek philosophy through the medieval world to the rise of the Medici, and the account terminates with the crowning of George III as King of England.

Beginning on page 224 is the following stimulating remark: "It was a few Summers ago, that GENIUS, HUMOUR and myself took this same Magistrate along with us to pass some Days at the Foot of a certain Hill called *Parnassas,* where we have a small Habitation, which we hold of the Ladies of the Manor, who are nine maiden Sisters." It would be difficult to ignore this obvious reference to the Lodge of the Nine Sisters and all that it implies.

On page 237 of Volume II is a veiled reference to relevant matters: "The Royal Club or Society (as it is called) founded by *Charles* Second, was, at first, filled with Men of real Science and Learning. WISDOM was an original Member, but of late Years he went so seldom amongst them, that they thought proper to expel him for non attendance. After the Expulsion of WISDOM, GENIUS was desirous of being chosen into this Society; and that he might not be rejected on Account of his peculiar Abilities, he was introduced to them as a grave Antiquary who had great Knowledge in Coins, Fossils and Cockleshells." Obviously, *genius* in this case represents Elias Ashmole, Esquire, who was the most distinguished antiquary of his time, a world-famous collector of coins, and an accumulator of fossils, shells, and other geological curiosa. *Wisdom,* of course, was Bacon, who originated the entire project of the Royal Society.

Between January 21, 1769, and January 21, 1772, an unknown man using the pseudonym of Junius wrote as a man personally outraged. The sins of Parliament weighed heavily upon his soul. He spoke for England, for the American colonies, and for the world. He defended the freedom of the press, attacked taxation without representation, and was a vigorous and belligerent champion of human rights. There can be no doubt that his pen advanced the cause of the American Revolution and created sympathy for the victims of bungling English politicians. It is not remarkable that *The Letters of Junius* gave inspiration and comfort to the cause of American independence. They were widely read in the colonies, and the solid judgment which these *Letters* contained influenced the thinking of Franklin, Jefferson, and Hancock. "Both liberty and property are precarious," writes Junius, "unless the possessors have sense and spirit enough to defend them. This is not the language of vanity. If I am a vain man, my gratification lies within a narrow circle. I am the sole depository of my own secret, and it shall perish with me."

Roderick Eagle contributed a curious observation concerning a possible association between Junius and the Baconian group. Eagle wrote that the first person so far recorded to name Bacon as the author of the Shakespeare plays was the Reverend James Wilmot, D.D. (1726-1808), who was rector of Barton-on-the-Heath, in Warwickshire, in 1785. This sober scholar of Trinity, Oxford, never married, and devoted his life to quiet scholarship. A short biography by him was published by his niece. She made no reference to his Shakespearean-Baconian interest, but did attribute to him *The Letters of Junius*. Eagle doubted that Dr. Wilmot was sufficiently close to the political situation of his time—he ministered in a remote hamlet—to have written the celebrated *Letters*, but suggested that he may have been a literary accomplice who transcribed the original to throw inquisitive persons, especially handwriting experts, into further confusion. Eagle adds: "I have an old engraving showing 'Junius' dressed as a clergyman. He is writing on a sheet of paper which bears the heading 'to the King'. On either side of him sit two men, one of whom is dictating. Under these portraits have been written 'Lord George Sackville' and 'Lord Chatham'." The same author suspected that Dr. Wilmot was the author of the book *The Story of the Learned Pig*, published anonymously in London in 1786. Only one

THE TRUE PORTRAIT OF AN UNKNOWN MAN
From an engraved title page of an early edition of *The Letters of Junius*.

copy of this little book concerned with the transmigrations of a highly talented hog has been discovered. In one of its incarnations, the hog claimed to have written the plays attributed to Shakespeare. The editor of the pig's narrative signed himself "Transmigratus."*

Early editions of *The Letters of Junius* are ornamented with curious vignettes which may be described as landmarks of a French Secret Society. The first edition of certain of Voltaire's writings are similarly adorned. Dr. Wilmot would have been forty-three years old when the elusive Lawrence published his *Common Sense*. Here again, two men, both obscure and contemporary, nourished the same and most singular opinions. It is reported that Dr. Wilmot burned all of his research material without having published any of his findings! The eighteenth century was less suitable for the perpetuation of secret enterprises than were the sixteenth and seventeenth centuries. The cases of Junius, Lawrence, and Transmigratus proved, however, that it was possible to conceal an identity with the assistance of the proper persons. Even during the American revolutionary period the public mind was inclined to ignore the mysterious and to accept appearance without question. Most historians have merely perpetuated popular tarditions and have sought no reasonable explanation for extraordinary events.

Freemasonry of the eighteenth century cannot be estimated in terms of the modern Order. Masonic scholars were still dabbling in the systems of ancient Mysteries which dominated classical antiquity. The esoteric side of the rites and symbols was impressive to scholarly minds, and the Masons regarded themselves as the responsible custodians of a vast project dedicated by earlier adepts to the emancipation of humanity from ignorance and tyranny. The obligations of the Mason became his principal allegiances. There was growing resentment in the colonies against the English Crown, and the local administration offended the thoughtful.

---

*See *Shakespeare, New Views for Old*.

Dedication to principles gained importance where there are few causes worth supporting. Masonry also successfully bridged many religious differences and discords. The Brethren could practice Christian principles without emphasizing theological differences, thus supplying a spiritual horizon necessary to offset the conflict of sects.

The second half of the eighteenth century was marked by broad but discreet circulation of philosophical knowledge. What Bacon had called "experiments of light" and "experiments of comfort" gained fashionable support. The sentiments of the French people were appropriately touched when Dr. Benjamin Franklin and Voltaire embraced each other with fraternal tenderness on the floor of the Lodge of the Nine Sisters. It was only natural that under Franklin's guidance this Lodge should have enlarged its scope to become a veritable university of world political philosophy.

The Lodge of the Nine Sisters, guided by the impressive scholarship of Court de Gébelin, was the most philosophical, mystical, and esoteric of the French Lodges. Its membership included such extremes as Prince Charles de Rohan and Monsieur Danton. Lafayette was, of course, involved, and in 1785 the Marquis also joined the Egyptian Masonry of Cagliostro and proclaimed his absolute confidence in the Grand Cophte. When Anton Mesmer arrived from Vienna with his theories of animal magnetism, Lafayette was one of his first customers.*

Speaking of John Paul Jones, the American naval hero, Gerald W. Johnson notes: "As he was a Mason, the famous Lodge of the Nine Sisters, which counted among its membership Voltaire, Helvetius the philosopher, and Houdon the sculptor, invited him to attend to be eulogized."† Jean Antoine Houdon has been described as "affected by the romantic frenzy of the times." His artistic accomplishments included portraitures of George Washington and the Count di Cagliostro.

*See *Revolution and Freemasonry,* by Bernard Fay.
†See *The First Captain.*

Dr. Benjamin Franklin was not only a devout Quaker, but also a most astute diplomat. Among Franklin's outstanding virtues was discretion, a quality indispensable to statesmen. It is extremely difficult to trace Franklin's associations with Secret Societies, although such are known to have existed. In his extensive *Autobiography*, there is not even mention of his membership in a Masonic Order, although he was active in the Fraternity, and published an edition of Anderson's *Constitutions*. During his travels in England and on the Continent, Franklin contacted many prominent liberals and was received by them with marks of esteem and fraternity. He was present in the Lodge of the Nine Sisters during the elaborate memorial services for Voltaire. At the time of the peace negotiations in France, the Doctor was attended by Lafayette.

The details of Franklin's Masonic connections have been drawn largely from contemporary correspondence. He was duly elected Master of the Masons of Philadelphia, and was regarded as the first Grand Master of Pennsylvania, possibly by authority derived from the Grand Lodge at London. The esteemed doctor was much given to secret assemblies. He contemplated the formation of a club to be called The Society of the Free and Easy, which was to be devoted to moral and ethical instructions for those who intended later to associate themselves with Freemasonry. With several young men, he was active in organizing a group called the Junto. The rules governing this society were later incorporated into the Philosophical Society of Philadelphia. Those aware of Franklin's connections with Secret Fraternities will find the following quotation of interest: "There seems to me at present to be a great occasion for raising a *United Party for Virtue*, by forming the virtuous and good men of all nations into a regular body, to be governed by suitable, good, and wise rules, which good and wise men may probably be more unanimous in their obedience to, than common people are to common laws. I at present think, that whoever attempts this aright, and is well qualified, cannot fail of pleasing God, and of meeting with success."

Mutual interests in curiosa and antiquities are said to have inspired the friendship between Franklin and Sir Hans Sloane, President of the Royal Society. Franklin also knew Sir William Herschel, and was popular in England in spite of the Revolutionary War. George III consoled himself over the loss of the American colonies because Herschel had recently named a planet in his honor. Franklin was acquainted with Mesmer and Cagliostro, but there is no evidence that he ever met Rousseau. This celebrated French philosopher was living in strict retirement, but he received a copy of Franklin's liturgy for a new religion, with pleasure. Franklin, equally polite, commended the influence of Rousseau's philosophy not only upon the European mind, but also among the American colonies.

Franklin was in contact with certain obscure gentlemen in the colonies, who took no obvious action in the formation of the American government, but were secretly advancing the cause. The Philadelphia printer acted as confidential agent for this group on numerous occasions. He traveled about, visiting here and there, and delivered messages and reports to interested parties. He was close to the ear of Thomas Jefferson, whose attainments were also highly diversified. It is regrettable that most of Jefferson's library and papers were destroyed when the British army sacked Washington in the War of 1812. Franklin was a link between the European Secret Societies and the American democratic experiment. The following incident is indicative of this association.

Robert Allen Campbell, in his curious and rare work, *Our Flag*, described a meeting which took place in Cambridge, Massachusetts, in the fall of 1775. A committee had been appointed to consider a design for a colonial flag. The committeemen were entertained in the home of a patriotic citizen. At that time, a gentleman, whose name was not once mentioned in the reports of the meeting, but was always referred to as "The Professor," was a guest in the house. He later shared his apartment with Dr. Franklin. The Professor was apparently in the prime of life, but referred casually to historical events of the previous century as though he had been present at the time. He carried with him an ironbound chest filled with rare books and ancient manuscripts. It was noted as remarkable that he was a vegetarian.

The Professor was introduced to the committeemen, Messrs. Lynch and Harrison and General Washington, as the group assembled for dinner. When Dr. Franklin was presented, The Professor was especially cordial, and as they shook hands there was "an instantaneous, a very apparent and a mutually gratified recognition." The Professor dominated the meeting, and his recommendations for the colonial flag were immediately accepted. There can be no doubt from his words that he was associated with Esoteric Societies. Later, on the evening of December 13, 1775, Dr. Franklin, General Washington, and The Professor "spent most of the night in earnest comparison concerning the momentous question in which they each and all had such vital interest." On this occasion the unknown gentleman predicted that the new American nation would soon take its place among the recognized governments of the

George Washington, at the age of sixty-four years, wearing Masonic sash and apron and the collar and jewel of Past Master of his lodge. (Painted from life.)

—FROM HAYDEN'S *WASHINGTON AND HIS MASONIC COMPEERS*

world. The identity of The Professor was never discovered, and there were no further references to him.

There is no documentary evidence known to be in existence regarding the initiation of General Lafayette or the Lodge in which he was raised. This uncertainty led the Grand Lodge of Pennsylvania to appoint a committee in 1824 to verify the facts. The investigation satisfied the committee that Brother General Marie Jean Paul Joseph Roche Yves Gilbert du Motier, Marquis de Lafayette, was a Mason in good standing, and he was enrolled as an honorary member of the R. W. Grand Lodge F.&A.M. of Pennsylvania. The Marquis revisited America in 1784, called upon General Washington at Mount Vernon, and on this occasion presented Washington with a beautiful white satin apron, elaborately embroidered with Masonic emblems in red, white, and blue, the handiworks of Madame, the Marquise de Lafayette. Washington wore this

—FROM HAYDEN'S *WASHINGTON AND HIS MASONIC COMPEERS*

Washington's Masonic apron, embroidered on white satin by Madame Lafayette, and presented in 1784.

apron when he was present at the Masonic ceremony on the occasion of the laying of the cornerstone of the District of Columbia.*

In 1782, on June 24, Lafayette was received into the Loge du Contrat Social in Paris, with the honors properly rendered the Masons of the higher grade. The register containing this report covered the period of 1775-89, and included such signatures as La Rochefoucauld, Rousseau, and St.-Germain. Lafayette was on terms of some intimacy with the Comte de St.-Germain, and while the Comte considered the young Marquis a rather impetuous youth, they were of one mind on larger issues. Lafayette is a direct link between the political societies of France and the young American government.

In *The Theosophist* (Madras, October 1883), the editor, probably H. P. Blavatsky, commented on an article, "Adepts and Politics." She writes: "Yet it is as certain though this conviction is merely a *personal* one, that several Brothers of the Rosy Cross—or 'Rosicrucians,' so-called—did take a prominent part in the American struggle for independence, as much as in the French Revolution during the whole of the past century. We have documents to that effect, and the proofs of it are in our possession. . . . it is our firm conviction based on historical evidence and direct inferences from many of the *Memoirs* of those days that the French Revolution is due to *one* Adept. It is that mysterious personage, now conveniently classed with other 'historical *charlatans*' (i.e., great men whose occult knowledge and powers shoot over the heads of the imbecile majority), namely, the Count de St.-Germain—who brought about the just outbreak among the paupers, and put an end to the selfish tyranny of the French kings—the 'elect, and the Lord's anointed.' And we know also that among the *Carbonari*—the precursors and pioneers

---

*See *Washington and His Masonic Compeers,* by Sidney Hayden, for details of Washington's Masonic association and activities.

of Garibaldi—there was more than one *Freemason* deeply versed in occult sciences and Rosicrucianism."

Anderson's *Constitution of Freemasonry* was published exactly one hundred years after the appearance of the great Shakespearean folio in 1623. In 1730, Daniel Coxe of New Jersey was appointed Provincial Grand Master of the provinces of New York, New Jersey, and Pennsylvania by his Grace, Thomas, Duke of Norfolk, Grand Master of the Premiere Grand Lodge of England. Benjamin Franklin became a Mason in 1731, and was Provisional Grand Master of Pennsylvania in 1734. George Washington took his first degree in the Lodge at Fredericksburg, Virginia, in 1752. The early American Lodges met in taverns or inns, and the first Masonic Temple in America was built in Boston in 1832. It cannot be learned that Thomas Paine was a Mason, although he wrote an essay dealing with the origin of Freemasonry. He attempted to trace the Fraternity to the Celtic Druids. Of Masonry, George Washington wrote in 1791: "Being persuaded a just application of the principles on which Free Masonry is founded, must be promotive of virtue and public prosperity, I shall always be glad to advance the interests of this Society and be considered by them a deserving brother."*

It is believed that the Boston Tea Party was arranged around a chowder supper at the home of the Bradlee brothers, who were Masons, and that mother Bradlee kept the water hot so that they could wash off the disguises. "Who were these 'Mohawks,' Sons of Liberty, in paint and gear?" asks Madison C. Peters. "Free Masons, members of St. Andrews Lodge, led by the Junior Warden, Paul Revere."†

As the relations between the colonies became more strained, it was inevitable that the Lodge rooms should become council chambers, where, protected by obligations of secrecy, men could freely discuss mat-

---
*Given in writing to the officers of St. Andrew's Lodge at Newport, Rhode Island.
†See *The Masons, Makers of America*.

ters which could not publicly be propagated. Here, also, they could learn that they had staunch supporting brethren in England and on the Continent. Freemasons among the leaders in the American cause against England included Putnam, Montgomery, Wayne, Sullivan, Revere, Lafayette, Kosciuszko, Baron de Kalb, and Count Polaski. Robert Morris is also mentioned. The Grand Master of the Masonic Lodges of France at that time was the Duke of Chartres, and the Duchess was the leader of the adoptive Lodge of women Freemasons. The head of another feminine Lodge was Madame Helvetius, Franklin's friend and hostess. The women's Lodge supplied John Paul Jones with funds for a ship. His famous vessel *Bon Homme Richard* was named in honor of Benjamin Franklin, in whose *Poor Richard's Almanac* Jones had read the maxim: "If you would have your business done, go yourself; if not, send."

The first Continental Congress, on the motion of George Washington, selected Peyton Randolph, past Grand Master of Masons of Virginia, to preside over its deliberations. Later, John Hancock, another Mason, succeeded him. It was Hancock who signed the Declaration of Independence with a signature so bold that "the King of England could read it without spectacles." It is believed that Thomas Jefferson became a Mason in France. Of the fifty-six signers of the Declaration of Independence, nearly fifty were Masons. Only one is known with certainty not to have been a member of the Order.

At Bunker Hill, on June 17, 1775, fell General Joseph Warren, Grand Master of the Massachusetts Grand Lodge. There is a report unverified that George Washington personally made Lafayette a Mason in military Lodge No. 19, at Morristown, New Jersey.

Frederick Wilhelm August Heinrich Ferdinand, Baron von Steuben, who received the first offer of surrender from Lord Cornwallis at Yorktown, was made a Mason in New York State. He had been aide-de-camp to the King of Prussia. Other Masonic leaders included General Nathaniel Green and Major General Henry Knox. All but two of Washington's Brigadier Generals were Masons, as was Ethan Allen of Green Mountain Boy fame. Of the fifty-five members of the Constitutional Convention, all but five were Masons.

The Latin American Patriots

The early colonization of the Latin American countries was dominated by the Spaniards, and the several colonies which they had established were governed by Spanish viceroys until the rise of the liberators. It is therefore useful to examine the condition of Secret Societies in Spain during the era of the conquest and the centuries which followed. The fate of Spain and the rapid decline of the power of that country was strongly influenced by the Inquisition. The Inquisition was established in Spain in 1233, but its original sphere of influence was largely confined to the kingdom of Aragon. Ferdinand and Isabella, remembered for their participation in the financing of Columbus, were directly responsible for the promotion of the Inquisitional program. About 1481, the queen brought the Inquisition to Castile, and two years later the notorious Torquemada was named Grand Inquisitor of Spain. For the eighteen years he filled this office, Torquemada averaged ten thousand executions annually.

While some of the victims of the Holy Office were sacrificed to the political ambitions of powerful families, the majority was accused of heresy. This convenient term seems to have been applied generously to those intellectuals whose mental horizons had been broadened by the educational institutions which flourished under the Moors. The heretics were the liberals, the progressives, and such as favored the rights of man. The secret association of spies, fanatics, and informers which served the Inquisitional Court were the agents of a determined effort to destroy the philosophers, scholars, and mystics who refused to be converted to the prevailing concept of salvation. The zeal and thoroughness of the Inquisitors implied that heretical tendencies were strong and that the Church was in a fair way to lose its control over the Spanish conscience. There was an abortive revolution against Charles V in 1520, when he attempted to limit the traditional liberties of his people. The Secret Society which was then led by Padilla was suppressed, but not destroyed. It reappeared in 1821 as the *Comuneros* (the Confederation of the Communists), a group dedicated to the overthrow of the Spanish monarchy. As this revival coincides closely with the revolutionary outbreaks among the Spanish colonials in America, more than a coincidence may be expected.

In 1726, the Grand Lodge of England granted a patent for the establishment of a Masonic Lodge at Gibraltar, and another was founded the following year at Madrid. The Inquisition, which still exercised considerable power, persecuted the Orders so diligently that the Spanish Masons were forced to adopt an elaborate program of secrecy. The Lodges, however, found temporary liberty and considerable opportunity for political activity during the confusion caused by the Napoleonic Wars. Masonry was later again suppressed by Ferdinand VII, so that such Lodges as continued to function concealed their activities under other names. The Grand Orient of Madrid was in secret correspondence with those French Lodges which were taking so large a part in the conditioning of the people of France. The Zoroastrian Rite attracted prominent members of the Spanish military, and it was always expedient to have friends in the army.

The Brazilian Emperor Dom Pedro I was elected Grand Master of the Grand Lodge of Brazil in 1825. Heckethorn notes that the turbulent republics of South America all had their Masonic Lodges, which were in many cases political clubs in disguise. The Grand Lodge of Mexico was instituted in 1825, but there was Masonic activity in that country prior to that date. The Masonic conviction of liberty, equality, and fraternity must have been attractive to progressive Catholics, for even priests associated themselves with the Lodges. Many prominent Latin Americans of the period of the revolution were educated in Europe or were in contact with enthusiasts returning to their homeland indoctrinated with the means and ends of the French Revolutionists.

With Secret Societies intensely active in Spain and Portugal, many royalists, though faithful children of the Church, privately associated themselves with concepts of liberalism which excited the imagination and appealed to the instinct of the adventurous. This drift of esoteric traditions from Spain was openly acknowledged during the Napoleonic Era, and, though later suppressed in the larger centers of population, continued to inflame afflicted classes in the Spanish colonies. Historical references, however, are meager due to the Inquisition, and even the heroes were reluctant to commit themselves to membership in organizations regarded as highly subversive by the Holy Office.

Nor should the secret traditions which lingered among the Indian tribes of the several regions be overlooked. The mystical and philosophical overtones of the European groups were in broad agreement with the occult religious teachings of the pre-Columbian priesthoods. Through a mingling of aspirations and convictions, the Creoles, mestizos, and Indians found not only a common ground, but were also inspired to a program of mutual support, protection, and, if necessary, concealment. These factors, though of slight interest to the literal historian, have fascination for the political psychologist. There are persistent reports that the Secret Societies of the Aztecs, Mayas, and Incas continued long after the conquest, guarded by those reticent aborigines who refused to renounce their ancient cultural institutions.

Although it may be difficult to trace the rumors, there are elusive reports identifying most of the political reformers of the Latin American countries with the Fraternities and Societies of the Indian tribes. Benito Juárez was suspected of such affiliations, and the followers of Pancho

Villa were outspoken on this subject. There are vast areas still comparatively unexplored south of the Rio Grande. The primitive religions are powerful in these regions; and wherever the old faiths survive, the esoteric doctrine is served and protected and the occult arts are cultivated.

Simon Bolívar

In the case of Simon Bolívar (1783-1830) is exemplified the effect of direct contact with the European Secret Societies. From his political prophecies, it is evident that Bolívar was not only a brilliant statesman, but also an intellectual liberal. He read extensively, and his favorite authors were Rousseau, Montesquieu, Hobbes, Helvetius, Holbach, Hume, and Spinoza. A man so naturally emotional, so strongly inclined toward mysticism, and at the same time so moved and dominated by internal pressures would naturally turn to philosophy for inspiration, guidance, and comfort. Though a devout Catholic, he was one of those Latin American heroes who refused to accept the reactionary tendencies of his Church.

Bolívar witnessed the coronation of Napoleon, but was less impressed by the imperial crown than by the tremendous personal influence which Bonaparte exercised over his followers. While in France and Italy, the Liberator contacted the various groups that were working quietly but relentlessly to accomplish the freedom of the human mind. The democratic ideology converted him completely, as is proved by his vow at Rome. On the occasion, Bolívar and his tutor, Simon Rodriquez, stood on the summit of the holy hill. Suddenly the young man fell on his knees and addressing Rodriquez, cried out: "I swear before you, I swear by the God of my forefathers, I swear by my forefathers, I swear by my native country, that I shall never allow my hands to be idle nor my soul to rest until I have broken the shackles which chain us to Spain."

It was during his European travel that Bolívar joined the Masonic

Order. Michael Vaucaire dramatizes the Masonic associations of the young man by an episode which occurred while Bolívar was in his stateroom at sea: "Bolívar came across his Freemason's diploma. He unrolled the great printed sheet, which showed a curtain hanging in an antique temple. It bore the different symbols, level, trowel, square, compass, the three points and the mallet, also crouching sphinxes. Bolívar recalled his introduction to the Lodge at Cadiz, whither he had been drawn by curiosity rather than conviction. He had taken oath to accept no legitimate government in his country save one elected by the full vote of the people, and, to strive with all his might to establish a republican system."* Later, in Paris, Bolívar was raised to Master in the Lodge of the Nine Sisters.

General Simon Bolívar.

There is a noble monument in the principal square of Caracas, his birthplace, which carries the bold words: "Simon Bolívar, Liberator of

*See *Bolívar, the Liberator*.

Venezuela, New Granada, Ecuador and Peru, and Founder of Bolivia." The United States viewed with deep sympathy the struggles of the Latin American countries. The stepson of George Washington sent to Bolívar, through Brother Lafayette, a miniature and medallion including a lock of Washington's hair as a token of esteem. But if General Bolívar enjoyed the sympathy of those who loved freedom, he also suffered deeply and cruelly for his convictions, like most who have served unselfishly to liberate their fellow men. He died a tired, broken old man at the age of forty-seven, as Ybarra writes: ". . . in exile, under an alien roof, clad in a borrowed nightshirt."*

The vision which the Liberator left to his people can be estimated from a few quotations: "America," said Bolívar in 1823, "is not a problem; neither is it a fact. It is the highest and most irrefutable assignment of destiny." In a document dated 1829, the Liberator wrote: "I have achieved no other good than independence. That was my mission. The nations I have founded will, after prolonged and bitter agony, go into an eclipse, but will later emerge as states of the one great republic, AMERICA."†

Miguel Hidalgo

The career of Hidalgo (1753–1811) emphasizes the prominence of certain political clubs built around liberal principles imported from the Secret Societies of Spain and the rise of local organizations to advance the cause of social justice in Mexico.

Under various protective pseudonyms, such as Protective Clubs, Literary Circles, and Social Enterprises, the spirit of liberty extended its

---
*See *Bolívar, the Passionate Warrior.*
†Quoted from *Simon Bolívar,* by Gerard Masur.

sphere of influence from the European Lodges of liberation to the valley of Mexico. The Masonic memberships of certain key figures involved in the Mexican struggle for independence should not be accepted as proof that these men were directly associated with esoteric organizations. The condition of Freemasonry at the time, however, and its place in the descent of the Great Plan for liberty, equality, and fraternity constitutes a tangible link between the Secret Schools of the ancient world with their moral and ethical convictions and the cause of human enlightenment which was so strongly championed by the great Mexican patriot.

The patronymic name Hidalgo (*hijo de algo*, which means *son of somebody*) infers a degree of aristocracy or minor nobility. Miguel Hidalgo, called the Father of Mexican Independence, was ordained to the priesthood in 1778, and from that time on was in frequent difficulties with his religious superiors. Though of slight stature and humble appearance, Hidalgo had improved his years at the Royal and Pontifical University of Mexico. He early showed an inclination for history and political science. Even as a young man, he dedicated his life to the emancipation of the Mexican people, especially the Indians. He favored the writings of the French rationalists, particularly the theories of Rousseau and Voltaire, as these applied to the rights of man. He was denounced to the Inquisition at Valladolid for unorthodoxy. He was accused of reading prohibited books and of favoring Jansenism. It was particularly pointed out that he carried with him in his wanderings a copy of the Koran.

Concerning the researches of the Inquisition, Arthur Howard Noll writes: "In the meantime the Holy Office had pursued an investigation by its usual methods, and had discovered that Hidalgo was developing revolutionary tendencies; that he was accustomed to speak of monarchs as tyrants, and that he cherished aspirations for political liberty. He had little respect for the *Index Expurgatorius*, and was so extensively read in current French literature that he had become thoroughly imbued with French ideas, or, as it was subsequently called, he was *afrancesado*. He had, by the direct evidence of thirteen witnesses sighted before the tribunal, been guilty of heretical utterances, sufficient to consign him to the stake."*

The officers of the Inquisition, however, admitted that there were some doubts on certain points, and to the amazement of Hidalgo himself the case against him was suspended and the evidence filed for future reference. It was referred to in due time. The principal heresy concerned Hidalgo's program for the economic and social improvement of the Indians and mestizos. He was ultimately deprived of his benefice, and by his forty-seventh year was completely dedicated to the liberation of his people from foreign tyranny and domestic oppression.

Of special interest was the sudden development throughout the provinces of what were called social and literary clubs. These sprang up rapidly, but no satisfactory history of their origin or the persons responsible for the idea are available. In some way, these groups eluded the Holy Office, and from their inception were dedicated to the same ends that dominated similar Secret Societies in Europe. In 1808, Hidalgo joined one of these clubs in Queretaro, immediately became its principal leader, and extended his influence through this chain of available organizations. This circumstance probably explains the well-authenticated report that Hidalgo became a member of the Masonic Fraternity in middle life despite the edicts of the Vatican. Gould, in his *Military Lodges,* stated positively that Jose Maria Morelos, another priest devoted to the cause of Hidalgo, was a Mason. He was also executed as an "unconfessed heretic." It was in one of these clubs that Hidalgo met Ignatio Allende, who later became the military genius of the revolution. The appearance of a network of Societies dedicated to the private conviction of political liberty may well witness a contact between European groups and the New World. Conditions in Spain were such as to justify a discreet program of organizations in Mexico.

*See *The Life and Times of Miguel Hidalgo y Costilla.*

Hidalgo's revolution was short-lived and his career as a leader of rebellion lasted only one year. Allende was executed on the 26th of June 1811. Hidalgo was first degraded by the ecclesiastical court and then turned over to the civil courts. He suffered the auto-da-fé, and on the 30th of July 1811, received a military execution. He met death heroically, and his last words were a prayer that heaven would favor the independence of his people. Although Hidalgo's name is revered throughout Mexico, little has been written about him which is available to his countrymen. The details of his career probably have been considered inflammatory and contrary to the present interests of the Church and State.

Benito Pablo Juárez

On the 21st of March, in a little Zapotecan Indian village of some twenty families, was born Benito Juárez (1806-1872), the emancipator of Mexico. He had no memory of his parents who died during his infancy, but, after numerous difficulties, succeeded in educating himself in law and became deeply involved in the political problems of his country. The policies of Juárez were brought to the attention of the United States by the London correspondent of the *New York Tribune,* an international exile by the name of Karl Marx. Juárez has been described as an agnostic, but a careful consideration of his attitudes reveals not a rebellion against God but against the theological institutions which burdened the people of Mexico. This silent, inscrutable Indian belonged to a race moved inwardly by powerful convictions, but outwardly impassive. His God was the Father of Freedom, served by a priesthood of liberators.

Juárez became a Mason in his youth. After the overthrow of the Maximilian Empire, Mexican Freemasonry was consolidated in 1868, Benito Juárez being one of its highest officials. *Mackey's History of Freemasonry* contains the following note: "It would seem as if the authority of Juárez alone held these Rites together, since at his death in

1872—although he was succeeded as President by his chief follower, Sebastian Lerdo de Tejeda, also a prominent Freemason—dissensions arose, and they fell asunder, Alfredo Chavero becoming Grand Master of the Grand Orient, and Jose Maria Mateos of the National Grand Lodge."*

General Francisco Javier Mina, another martyr to Mexican liberty, was a Freemason. Ignacio Comonfort, also a member of the Fraternity, was Secretary of War under President Alvarez and later was acting President of the Republic. He took an active part against the French invasion, but was killed by bandits or irregular troops in 1863.

General Porfirio Diaz was an early supporter of Juárez, under whose influence he became a member of the Masonic Fraternity. He attained the 33° and was Sovereign Grand Commander of the Supreme Council of Mexico for many years. He was succeeded by his friend, General Manuel Gonzales, 33°, in 1880. Diaz was elected President in 1884 and remained in office until his resignation in 1911. General Mariano Escobedo, a close friend of Juárez and Diaz, was also a Mason and a member of the Supreme Council of Mexico.†

Recent Mystical Movements

The recent activities of the older Secret Societies, with one or two notable exceptions, is difficult to trace. Numerous Orders, Fraternities, Societies, and cults have come into existence, many claiming an honorable antiquity, but few in a position to prove their claims to those of scholarly inclination. These recent movements may be broadly considered as revivals of old learning, but when their pretensions are seriously investigated, the findings are inconclusive. For this reason it seems wiser to refrain from passing judgment upon any of them. Even the most sincere

*See revised edition by Robert Ingham Clegg, 33°.
†See *Montana Mason*, Feb. 1922, article "Masonry in Mexico."

efforts to clarify the situation would result in unfortunate animosities. Those addicted to the numerous sects are generally more devout than analytical, and nothing would be gained by offending the devotees of any religious persuasion.

The difficulty of tracing historical descents is also increased by the innumerable divisions which arose in the American religious life. The rise of science undermined the larger institutions of theology and induced thoughtful persons to seek spiritual consolation in movements offering broader and deeper interpretations of rituals and dogmas. As the demand increased, the supply correspondingly enlarged until the boundaries of orthodoxy lost definition. The nineteenth-century intellectual became a freethinker, convinced that his own judgment was superior to that of the clergy. The freethinker was neither an agnostic nor an atheist; he was a liberal, convinced that freedom included the privilege of questioning authority, both sacred and profane. Emancipation, however, was a mixed blessing. It was one thing to escape old superstitions, and quite another thing to be wise enough not to fall into new errors. Many beliefs that flourished for a time were slight improvements, but had the virtue of being different, if not better.

As may be expected, there was a luxurious growth of absurd notions. They flourished upon the prevailing ignorance, but having no roots in good soil, these parasitical cults were fascinating but ineffective. The more bizarre were short-lived or survived only at the expense of the credulous. Substantially, the citizens of the nineteenth century received as a legacy the principles and convictions of the eighteenth-century political societies. The Age of Reason had secured the rights of man. It then remained for education to provide the machinery required to protect those rights. Democracy had emerged as fact, but the fact was not sufficient. The theory of freedom could be preserved by Secret Societies, but the practice of freedom required the cooperation of an enlightened people dedicated to a lofty ethical standard.

When evaluating the esoteric groups of this period, the most reliable guide is their acceptance of the responsibility of the Great Plan. Progress is not ordinarily for the advancement of the individual, but for the unfoldment of the universal project. The real Esoteric Schools still labor toward the goal of the World Commonwealth. The Plan remains utopian, and the disciple advancing through the grades of a legitimate initiate-system is being prepared, not for personal emancipation, but as an instrument for the liberation of his fellow men. Wherever religious inducements are personal and selfish or the devotee is encouraged to advance his own growth without consideration for others, there is something wrong with the policy of the sect. Yet, the literature of modern metaphysical movements seldom emphasizes growth as responsibility. The reader is encouraged to study mystical systems or to affiliate with organizations claiming extraordinary knowledge in the hope that he will acquire the skill to advance his own condition. Where such objectives are used to intrigue the gullible, those of sincere mind and heart are entitled to reservations.

The old Secret Societies remain as they had always been, custodians of an overconviction. They are now emphasizing the right use of privileges. Education can be conferred by schools and universities, but enlightenment must still result from internal growth. Without the proper development of his superphysical resources, the individual cannot protect his physical rights and privileges. Progress of society always demands that the human being as a person be in advance of the institutions which he creates. When leadership passes to the keeping of external enterprises, the person becomes a slave to his own project. This is not the Plan, and if the condition continues uncorrected, physical society will collapse upon the individual, burying him beneath the debris of his own productions.

With the rise of materialism, the Secret Societies were concealed from the profane, not by any elaborate machinery of their own, but by popular disbelief. There was no place for sacred institutions in minds already dedicated to scientific skepticism. The importance of invisible principles over visible purposes and ambitions was simply ignored. Only that small minority which remained true to a higher standard of values continued to be concerned with inevitable outcome. For the majority, the physical world with its wonders was sufficient to absorb all available time and interest. The result is obvious. The physical state of man enlarged, and his ethical horizons were appropriately narrowed.

The old adversaries were gone. The power of the Church and State to plague the destiny of the average man was broken. It was no longer needful to struggle against the despotism of feudalism or the perversities of princes. The Inquisition had lost its terror, and theology was unable to impose its traditional formulas upon a downtrodden laity. But the ills that men must bear changed their appearances, not their substance. The authority of science took the place left vacant by the departing authorities of aristocracy and theology. It was still necessary for the human spirit to struggle against the intolerances of the human mind.

Personal ambitions, liberated by the new code of freedom, immediately began to dream of supremacy. A vast concept, highly competitive in principle and highly destructive in practice, perpetuated most of the instruments of the old tyranny. Siegfried had slain the dragon, but was in grave danger of being drowned in the blood that flowed from the mortal wound. Having overcome the despotism of entrenched classes, humanity discovered the despotism in itself. It was faced with the unhappy realization that tyrannical systems are only symbols of those tyrannical instincts which exist in all creatures until they are overcome by enlightened understanding.

It is evident that the continued operations of the genuine Secret Societies make it unwise to describe them or identify their members. Humanity has not yet reached a state of collective security in which leadership beyond the political sphere is unnecessary. The need for

AMERICA'S ASSIGNMENT WITH DESTINY

THE REVERSE OF THE GREAT SEAL
Professor Charles Eliot Norton of Harvard described the design thus: "The device adopted by Congress is practically incapable of effective treatment; it can hardly (however artistically treated by the designer) look otherwise than as a dull emblem of a Masonic fraternity." This is one of the important esoteric landmarks that have been conveniently ignored.

—FROM HUNT'S *HISTORY OF THE SEAL OF THE UNITED STATES*

guidance actually increases with the complexity of mundane affairs. All of sincere heart find consolation in the conviction that powers beyond and above human corruption continue to administer the destiny of the globe. It would be a mistake to confuse this governing body with the various sects which pretend to authority, but give no indications or proof that they can manage efficiently even their own affairs.

Those sensitive to subtle values will find positive indications of fortuitous intervention if they care to seek for them. The landmarks are not obvious to the profane, but years of familiarity with the proportions of the project enable the thoughtful to recognize the systematic unfoldment of the Great Plan. The truth is more obvious among those peoples whose religions acknowledge the existence of an invisible government. This has always been concealed in the descent of the Western Mystery religion.

Once Christianity had rejected paganism, it refused to recognize the Esoteric Orders of the pre-Christian world. It regarded them as detrimental to its own prestige, and sought relentlessly to exterminate them. This was impossible, but the Church refused to accept and to teach a universal religion or a universal philosophy. The spiritual mysteries of life belong to no one faith, race, or school. In order to advance itself as the supreme custodian of salvation, ecclesiasticism had to reject the Mystery system. In doing so, it did not destroy that system, but forfeited its own place as an instrument for the fulfillment of the Great Plan. In its effort to usurp this high destiny for itself, the Church obscured the very essentials of human progress and discouraged its followers from those noble and unselfish convictions which might long ago have supplied the incentives for a Universal Reformation of mankind.

When legitimate authority passed from the Church to the Orders of the Quest, this secret ecclesia drew to itself those who truly loved mankind. Even with the passing of centuries, the rift has not been mended. Theological groups still emphasize a personal salvation achieved by miraculous means. In this case, the very word *miraculous* stands for the rejected esoteric tradition. It is the undefined and, for the theological, undefinable science of human regeneration. It is not sufficient to say that beyond the Church is only the unknown sphere of God. Actually, beyond the Church are the Mysteries, guarded by the shepherds of men. There is nothing that can limit the merit of present action more completely than lack of vision about accumulative consequences of action. Humanity can release itself from defeatism only when the true proportions of the Great Plan are at least partly perceived. The lack of the realization of high purpose contributes to the cultivation of less desirable motives and inclinations.

The Secret Societies are now engaged upon a broad reformation of the world-educational concept. The great universities and schools must fulfill the destiny which conceived them and sustained them through long and troublous times. Humanity cannot be preserved by the three "R's," unless the universal truths locked within the forms of the arts and sciences are released. Just as mysticism once opened and revealed the secrets of religion, so it must now open and reveal the secrets of the sciences. Forms must give up the spirits locked within them, otherwise the seeds cannot grow and bear their proper fruit. The great tree, which is knowledge, with its twelve branches, is for the healing of the nations. Who shall say that it has revealed the fullness of its benefits?

The forces opposing the essential progress of humanity are always embodiments of the three great enemies: ignorance, superstition, and fear. As man advances in his collective evolution, these negative obstacles supply a necessary incentive for individual improvement toward collective security. Ignorance is the state of insufficient knowledge. The concept is relative, but sufficient knowledge is that which is superior to whatever circumstances may prevail. Superstition is addiction to that which is untrue. The prevailing superstition is the acceptance of materialism, an acceptance which is indefensible and undemonstrable. Fear is man's anxiety over the consequences of his own actions, becoming the victim of the collective conduct of his own kind. Until every possible interpretation of the qualities of the three adversaries have been exhausted, the work of human enlightenment must continue.

In each generation, the adept-teacher must be out of sympathy with the prevailing abuses. He must always oppose entrenched corruption and strive against what has been called the static of masses. Human behavior corrupted by false doctrines resents its own benefactors. The Secret Societies are champions of progress through constructive change, but men fear change and doubt progress. Destiny, however, conspires against the permanence of insufficient institutions. Growth is natural to the wise, and inevitable for the foolish. Conditions beyond human control are forever breaking down the limitations which man has placed upon his own future. Destiny and the Mysteries must win, for they are on the side of the Great Plan.

As that which is necessary always provides the means for supplying its own necessity, the human state proves the esoteric tradition. It is not conceivable that there should be laws in space for which there are no channels of release in human society. Truth always comes to man through man. The great initiate-teachers have offered their own souls as channels for the distribution of cosmic truths. These teachers are not only unselfish, they are also adequate for the ministry which is their chosen task.

Through long periods of discipleship, they have become learned in statescraft, in law, medicine, art, literature, and science. In their natures, philosophy and mysticism have been unfolded far beyond the understanding of the profane. Obviously, the Great Schools, functioning through their trained and appointed messengers, constitute the highest leadership available to man or required by man. In order, however, that their work be accomplished it is not sufficient that they have the needed vision. This vision must be communicated. It must be extended throughout human society until humanity redeems itself by the experience of enlightenment. The security that the world seeks cannot be bestowed; it must be earned. When a sufficient number has attained this degree of true leadership, the imperishable democracy of the sages will become a fact in the mortal sphere.

The genuine Esoteric Associations always required that disciples prepare themselves for careers of practical service. The student was expected to attain to a state of unusual skill or proficiency in some branch of learning. He was then to practice this profession or craft as a means of extending his sphere of constructive influence. He was to teach through example, enriching his chosen vocation with the overtones of enlightened religious philosophy. Thus, gradually creating a significant zone of influence, he was available for whatever task the Keepers of the Great Plan required. Practical ends can only be achieved by practical means, and the agents of the Universal Reformation must be sufficient for every emergency.

Rather than attempt to indicate modern organizations which may or may not be instruments of the Mystery system, it is more useful to recommend that each truth seeker make use of his own faculties of discrimination. The Esoteric Orders have never accepted candidates without reasonable qualifications, nor have they offered any inducements except the privilege of becoming unselfish, useful, and humble. They have never promised to gratify the whims of mortals, and have reserved the right to select in their own way those whom they believed to have the courage, the insight, and the fortitude which the magnitude of the project demanded. Human society cannot be preserved by Fraternities of the unfit, even though the members be well-intentioned. Successful leaders in various materialistic fields usually lack qualifications essential for discipleship in the Secret Schools. Those aspiring to become initiate-teachers must discipline and improve their abilities before their candidacy can be considered.

Those initiates of the Western descent whose names are known convey a fair impression of acceptable qualifications. Such men as Roger Bacon, Francis of Assisi, Dante, Paracelsus Basil Valentine, Robert Fludd, Francis Bacon, and St.-Germain immediately recall the remarkable abilities, the wonderful devotion, and the enduring fortitude of those who resolved to devote their lives to the improvement of mankind. Quiet thinking will dissolve all doubts as to the genuine teachings of the Mystery Schools and the qualifications necessary to membership. Usually, the Schools selected their disciples, imposing upon them rules of discrimination and discretion, so that no matter of importance was entrusted to anyone still plagued by his own ambitions or likely to succumb to the temptations of worldly acclaim.

The principal test of existing religious and mystical organizations is,

—FROM AN EIGHTEENTH-CENTURY HERMETIC BOOK

A SYMBOLICAL PRINTER'S DEVICE
This vignette is a pictorial signature of the Secret Societies of Liberty.

therefore, their practical acceptance of collective responsibility. If the group is concerned primarily with the perpetuation of its own abstract doctrines and has provided no means for the direct application of these doctrines for the advancement of all men, something is wrong. Wisdom is not destined for the few. Certainly, it must be given to a few, that through them it may be taught to the many. Any group which imposes artificial limitations of prejudice, bigotry, or intellectual exclusiveness frustrates the legitimate program of universal enlightenment. No one religion, philosophy, sect, or creed will ever be the sole custodian of the esoteric tradition. Organizations pretending to provide the "only hope of salvation" can be immediately discarded. The Great Plan has taken on innumerable appearances that meet the requirements of human evolution, but the Plan itself is beyond all appearances. Many have the privilege of serving, but only the divine wisdom itself has the authority to dogmatize, and it has never indulged that prerogative.

The design is not difficult to visualize if the mind and heart are properly receptive. The religions, philosophies, sciences, and arts of mankind are all ensouled organisms. They grow up in the world, like flowers in a field, all nourished by the same light and moisture. It profits nothing to argue as to which of these flowers is the fairest or which is the most likely to survive, nor is it more practical to debate such issues as which shrub was predestined to govern the others. All are channels for the one life, which alone determines the fulfillment of the processes of growth. The separate organisms of learning must finally come together to form one vast organization. If one part be lacking, the body will be imperfect. Who shall say in a magnificent association of this kind that any of the fragments which form the perfect whole is unessential? Remember, the Great League of Learning is a democratic commonwealth and not an autocracy of the elect. The Great League is the fruit of the Great Plan. Once the body of knowledge has been ordered by the canons of esoteric architecture, it becomes one vast sanctuary. It is the temple built without hands—the Everlasting House. Into this body the Great Plan incarnates, so that the form itself, built by men through love and consecration, is ensouled with the immortal light of the Mystery tradition.

There are two motions in human society. One is toward *understanding,* and this is the unifying force. The other motion is toward *misunderstanding,* and this is the dividing force. Each human being advances the universal destiny to the degree that he overcomes within himself the impulses to divide and separate. It is not always possible to defend the conduct of groups or individuals or to cooperate with that which is obviously perverse. Too often, however, division is due simply to prejudice or to those egocentric impulses which tend to isolation through a false conviction of personal superiority. All institutions, sacred and secular, are composed of human beings. As these grow and unfold their natural consciousness, they verge toward each other by simple convictions of fraternity. Every possible effort should be made to encourage good feeling between sincere persons of different beliefs. This is only possible when all are generous and find justification in the realization of the pressing need of united effort.

The pages of history reveal the irresistible unifying force operating in human affairs. The story of man is the record of the struggle upward and forward from isolation to unification. No one can go against this motion without betraying himself, his world, and his God. All good things have come to those who have learned to work together, for this simple procedure is a symbol of civilization. Cooperation is the Great Work, the social alchemy which produces the Universal Medicine. It is recommended that the sincere truth seeker examine the various organizations which have risen in human society, and determine by their works rather than by their pretensions which ones are dedicated to the advancement of World Fraternity. Such associations, whether they be actual instruments of the Secret Schools or simply groups of sincere persons, are laboring in the light and for the light. Once convinced of the reality of the

Great Plan, the individual also receives a vision of realities which enable him to conduct his own affairs in harmony with the larger destiny. The esoteric tradition, first embodied in its adepts and later incarnated in the whole body of humankind, brings the kingdom of heaven to the earth. A regenerated human society, unfolding under the disciples of the Mysteries, fashions the Eternal City, which bears witness to the laws of heaven. Who shall deny that this vision of things possible to man is the noblest and most wonderful of human dreams? And who shall deny that man has within himself the power to make his dreams come true? Progress builds solid foundations under dreams. The trestle board of the Mysteries is the divine dream for humanity. The Mystery Schools were the sacred colleges, and the first graduates of those secret institutions were the adept-builders. These initiate-builders were skilled in the arts and sciences required to transform the dream of universal brotherhood into the temporal fact of the divine commonwealth. The initiate Jesus, personifying the Great Plan, declared its simple rule when he said: "He that is not with me is against me. . . ." (Matt. 17:30).